MAD LIBS®

MONSTER MASH
MAD LIBS

by Tristan Roarke

INSTRUCTIONS

MAD LIBS® is a game for people who don't like games! It can be played by one, two, three, four, or forty.

• RIDICULOUSLY SIMPLE DIRECTIONS

In this tablet you will find stories containing blank spaces where words are left out. One player, the READER, selects one of these stories. The READER does not tell anyone what the story is about. Instead, he/she asks the other players, the WRITERS, to give him/her words. These words are used to fill in the blank spaces in the story.

• TO PLAY

The READER asks each WRITER in turn to call out a word—an adjective or a noun or whatever the space calls for—and uses them to fill in the blank spaces in the story. The result is a MAD LIBS® game.

When the READER then reads the completed MAD LIBS® game to the other players, they will discover that they have written a story that is fantastic, screamingly funny, shocking, silly, crazy, or just plain dumb—depending upon which words each WRITER called out.

• EXAMPLE (*Before* and *After*)

"_____!" he said _____
     EXCLAMATION   ADVERB

as he jumped into his convertible _____ and
              NOUN

drove off with his _____ wife.
     ADJECTIVE

"___OUCH___!" he said ___HAPPILY___
     EXCLAMATION   ADVERB

as he jumped into his convertible ___CAT___ and
              NOUN

drove off with his ___BRAVE___ wife.
     ADJECTIVE

In case you have forgotten what adjectives, adverbs, nouns, and verbs are, here is a quick review:

An ADJECTIVE describes something or somebody. *Lumpy*, *soft*, *ugly*, *messy*, and *short* are adjectives.

An ADVERB tells how something is done. It modifies a verb and usually ends in "ly." *Modestly*, *stupidly*, *greedily*, and *carefully* are adverbs.

A NOUN is the name of a person, place, or thing. *Sidewalk*, *umbrella*, *bridle*, *bathtub*, and *nose* are nouns.

A VERB is an action word. *Run*, *pitch*, *jump*, and *swim* are verbs. Put the verbs in past tense if the directions say PAST TENSE. *Ran*, *pitched*, *jumped*, and *swam* are verbs in the past tense.

When we ask for A PLACE, we mean any sort of place: a country or city (*Spain*, *Cleveland*) or a room (*bathroom*, *kitchen*).

An EXCLAMATION or SILLY WORD is any sort of funny sound, gasp, grunt, or outcry, like *Wow!*, *Ouch!*, *Whomp!*, *Ick!*, and *Gadzooks!*

When we ask for specific words, like a NUMBER, a COLOR, an ANIMAL, or a PART OF THE BODY, we mean a word that is one of those things, like *seven*, *blue*, *horse*, or *head*.

When we ask for a PLURAL, it means more than one. For example, *cat* pluralized is *cats*.

MAD LIBS® is fun to play with friends, but you can also play it by yourself! To begin with, DO NOT look at the story on the page below. Fill in the blanks on this page with the words called for. Then, using the words you have selected, fill in the blank spaces in the story.

Now you've created your own hilarious MAD LIBS® game!

MONSTERS, OH MY!

NOUN _____

ADJECTIVE _____

TYPE OF LIQUID _____

SOMETHING ALIVE (PLURAL) _____

ANIMAL (PLURAL) _____

PLURAL NOUN _____

ADVERB _____

ARTICLE OF CLOTHING (PLURAL) _____

NUMBER _____

OCCUPATION (PLURAL) _____

NOUN _____

VERB ENDING IN "ING" _____

VERB _____

PLURAL NOUN _____

NOUN _____

VERB ENDING IN "ING" _____

OCCUPATION _____

MAD☺LIBS®

MONSTERS, OH MY!

Have you ever heard a loud _____ in the middle of
                                    NOUN

the night, when the moon is _____? Do you suspect
                                ADJECTIVE

your new neighbor might like to drink the _____
                                              TYPE OF LIQUID

from _____? Undead zombies, howling
        SOMETHING ALIVE (PLURAL)

were-_____, and vampires that sleep in _____
        ANIMAL (PLURAL)   PLURAL NOUN

have _____ scared the _____ off
        ADVERB   ARTICLE OF CLOTHING (PLURAL)

audiences for over _____ years. But what if these terrifying
                        NUMBER

_____ were real? What if they really *were* hiding under
OCCUPATION (PLURAL)

your _____, waiting until you're _____ before
        NOUN   VERB ENDING IN "ING"

they sneak out and _____ you? Luckily, monsters are just
                        VERB

a figment of our _____. So next time you hear that
                    PLURAL NOUN

_____ in the night, relax! You're just _____
NOUN   VERB ENDING IN "ING"

things. There's no _____ under your bed, waiting to get
                        OCCUPATION

you . . . or is there?!

MAD LIBS® is fun to play with friends, but you can also play it by yourself! To begin with, DO NOT look at the story on the page below. Fill in the blanks on this page with the words called for. Then, using the words you have selected, fill in the blank spaces in the story.

Now you've created your own hilarious MAD LIBS® game!

MAN'S BEST FRIEND

ADJECTIVE _____

OCCUPATION _____

CELEBRITY _____

SOMETHING ALIVE _____

VERB (PAST TENSE) _____

PART OF THE BODY (PLURAL) _____

TYPE OF FOOD _____

VERB _____

NOUN _____

ADJECTIVE _____

SILLY WORD _____

VEHICLE _____

A PLACE _____

PART OF THE BODY _____

EXCLAMATION _____

NOUN _____

VERB _____

MAD LIBS®

MAN'S BEST FRIEND

Ever wonder what it's like to have a/an _____ zombie as a
ADJECTIVE

best _____? Well, wonder no more, because my best friend,
OCCUPATION

_____, is a real-life zombie. Of course, she wasn't *always* a
CELEBRITY

zombie. She used to be a regular _____ before that other
SOMETHING ALIVE

zombie _____ on her leg. Being friends with a zombie
VERB (PAST TENSE)

sure does keep you on your _____. I need to keep
PART OF THE BODY (PLURAL)

lots of fresh _____ close by to feed my zombie friend so she
TYPE OF FOOD

won't try to _____ my _____. And our conversations
VERB   NOUN

aren't very _____ since my zombie friend usually just moans,
ADJECTIVE

"_____." At least she still likes to ride her _____
SILLY WORD   VEHICLE

around (the) _____. Although, every time she rides over a
A PLACE

bump, her _____ falls off and she yells, "_____!"
PART OF THE BODY   EXCLAMATION

But no matter what, she's still my best _____ friend
NOUN

forever . . . even if she's always trying to _____ on me.
VERB

From MONSTER MASH MAD LIBS® • Copyright © 2021 by Penguin Random House LLC

MAD LIBS® is fun to play with friends, but you can also play it by yourself! To begin with, DO NOT look at the story on the page below. Fill in the blanks on this page with the words called for. Then, using the words you have selected, fill in the blank spaces in the story.

Now you've created your own hilarious MAD LIBS® game!

HOW TO MAKE A MONSTER

ADJECTIVE _____

SOMETHING ALIVE _____

A PLACE _____

ADJECTIVE _____

PLURAL NOUN _____

PART OF THE BODY (PLURAL) _____

NUMBER _____

PART OF THE BODY (PLURAL) _____

TYPE OF BUILDING _____

NOUN _____

NOUN _____

NOUN _____

VERB ENDING IN "ING" _____

OCCUPATION _____

EXCLAMATION _____

VERB _____

PERSON IN ROOM _____

ADJECTIVE _____

MAD LIBS®

HOW TO MAKE A MONSTER

Hello, all my little _____ scientists! Dr. Frankenslime here
                          ADJECTIVE

to teach you how to make your own scary _____. The
                                         SOMETHING ALIVE

first thing you need to do is go to a creepy _____ with a/an
                                              A PLACE

_____ shovel and dig up all the _____ you
ADJECTIVE   PLURAL NOUN

need for the project. Don't feel like you have to give your monster

two _____ and two legs. If you want to give it
    PART OF THE BODY (PLURAL)

_____ _____ instead, go for it! This is your
NUMBER   PART OF THE BODY (PLURAL)

monster! Assemble all the parts in the laboratory inside your haunted

_____. If you don't have a lab, you can always use the
TYPE OF BUILDING

_____ in your own home instead. Once your monster is
NOUN

assembled, use an electrical _____ to bring it to life. A/An
                              NOUN

_____-storm is an excellent source of electricity due to all
NOUN

the lightning bolts _____ from the sky. When your
                    VERB ENDING IN "ING"

_____ first sits up, it may shout, "_____!" and
OCCUPATION   EXCLAMATION

_____ uncontrollably, but you must stay calm. Now all you
VERB

have to do is give it a name, like "_____," and go show the
                                    PERSON IN ROOM

world your _____ creation!
           ADJECTIVE

MAD LIBS® is fun to play with friends, but you can also play it by yourself! To begin with, DO NOT look at the story on the page below. Fill in the blanks on this page with the words called for. Then, using the words you have selected, fill in the blank spaces in the story.

Now you've created your own hilarious MAD LIBS® game!

VAMPIRE CLASS

SILLY WORD _____

ADJECTIVE _____

NOUN _____

NOUN _____

TYPE OF CONTAINER _____

ADVERB _____

PLURAL NOUN _____

SOMETHING ALIVE _____

PART OF THE BODY _____

TYPE OF LIQUID _____

ANIMAL _____

PART OF THE BODY (PLURAL) _____

OCCUPATION _____

EXCLAMATION _____

PLURAL NOUN _____

SOMETHING ALIVE _____

PART OF THE BODY (PLURAL) _____

MAD LIBS®

VAMPIRE CLASS

Velcome to Count _____'s class on how to be a successful
SILLY WORD

vampire! These _____ tips vill tell you everythink you need
ADJECTIVE

to know about being a creature of the _____ .
NOUN

Tip #1: Vampires hate the _____ , so never leave your
NOUN

_____ during the day. One step into the sunlight and
TYPE OF CONTAINER

you'll be _____ turned into a pile of _____ .
ADVERB   PLURAL NOUN

Tip #2: Before you bite your _____ on the _____ ,
SOMETHING ALIVE   PART OF THE BODY

say, "I vant to suck your _____ !"
TYPE OF LIQUID

Tip #3: To transform into a flying _____ , just raise your
ANIMAL

_____ into the air and say the _____ 's
PART OF THE BODY (PLURAL)   OCCUPATION

phrase, "_____ ."
EXCLAMATION

You are all excellent _____ ! Next, I vill teach you how to
PLURAL NOUN

hypnotize your _____ with your _____ .
SOMETHING ALIVE   PART OF THE BODY (PLURAL)

MAD LIBS® is fun to play with friends, but you can also play it by yourself! To begin with, DO NOT look at the story on the page below. Fill in the blanks on this page with the words called for. Then, using the words you have selected, fill in the blank spaces in the story.

Now you've created your own hilarious MAD LIBS® game!

WHAT LURKS IN LOCH NESS?

ADJECTIVE _____

NOUN _____

CELEBRITY _____

NUMBER _____

OCCUPATION _____

PERSON IN ROOM _____

SAME CELEBRITY _____

EXCLAMATION _____

ADJECTIVE _____

PLURAL NOUN _____

PART OF THE BODY _____

NUMBER _____

PLURAL NOUN _____

ADJECTIVE _____

ANIMAL _____

SILLY WORD _____

NOUN _____

ADJECTIVE _____

MAD LIBS®
WHAT LURKS IN LOCH NESS?

If you ever travel to Scotland, you might be _____ enough to

ADJECTIVE

catch a glimpse of the Loch Ness _____, also affectionately

NOUN

known as _____ . Sightings of the creature date all the way

CELEBRITY

back to the year _____ when, legend has it, a/an _____

NUMBER OCCUPATION

named _____ saw _____ rising from the lake and

PERSON IN ROOM SAME CELEBRITY

shouted, "_____!" Since then, Loch Ness has been a/an

EXCLAMATION

_____ destination for _____ traveling from all

ADJECTIVE PLURAL NOUN

over the world. The creature is said to have a/an _____

PART OF THE BODY

nearly _____ feet tall and a body longer than twenty

NUMBER

_____! While many think the legend is just a/an

PLURAL NOUN

_____ hoax, believers say the creature is actually some type of

ADJECTIVE

_____ that was trapped in the lake during the _____

ANIMAL SILLY WORD

age. Whatever the truth may be, if you're lucky enough to take a photo

of the _____ , you'll become one of the most _____

NOUN ADJECTIVE

people in the world!

MAD LIBS® is fun to play with friends, but you can also play it by yourself! To begin with, DO NOT look at the story on the page below. Fill in the blanks on this page with the words called for. Then, using the words you have selected, fill in the blank spaces in the story.

Now you've created your own hilarious MAD LIBS® game!

ARE YOU MY MUMMY?

ADJECTIVE _____

PLURAL NOUN _____

TYPE OF BUILDING _____

ARTICLE OF CLOTHING (PLURAL) _____

NOUN _____

NOUN _____

ADJECTIVE _____

PART OF THE BODY (PLURAL) _____

NOUN _____

SOMETHING ALIVE (PLURAL) _____

SILLY WORD _____

VERB _____

ADJECTIVE _____

TYPE OF CONTAINER _____

ANIMAL (PLURAL) _____

NUMBER _____

NOUN _____

MAD LIBS

ARE YOU MY MUMMY?

Is your mom a/an _____ mummy? Answer these helpful

ADJECTIVE

_____ to find out!

PLURAL NOUN

- Does your mom sleep inside a stone _____ while

TYPE OF BUILDING

  wrapped in _____?

ARTICLE OF CLOTHING (PLURAL)

- Does your mom come from a/an _____ in the middle

NOUN

  of a desert, where she creates _____ -storms by waving

NOUN

  around a/an _____ staff?

ADJECTIVE

- Does your mom keep her _____ in a/an

PART OF THE BODY (PLURAL)

  _____ by her bed?

NOUN

- When your _____ meet your mom, do they

SOMETHING ALIVE (PLURAL)

  scream, "_____!" and _____ in fear?

SILLY WORD   VERB

- Does your mom have a pile of _____ treasure in your

ADJECTIVE

  _____?

TYPE OF CONTAINER

- After your mom hugs you, are you covered in scarab

  _____?

ANIMAL (PLURAL)

If you answered "yes" to more than _____ of these questions,

NUMBER

your mom might be a/an _____!

NOUN

MAD LIBS® is fun to play with friends, but you can also play it by yourself! To begin with, DO NOT look at the story on the page below. Fill in the blanks on this page with the words called for. Then, using the words you have selected, fill in the blank spaces in the story.

Now you've created your own hilarious MAD LIBS® game!

DIARY FROM
THE BLACK LAGOON

ADJECTIVE _____

SOMETHING ALIVE (PLURAL) _____

ADJECTIVE _____

SILLY WORD _____

PLURAL NOUN _____

EXCLAMATION _____

COLOR _____

PLURAL NOUN _____

PART OF THE BODY (PLURAL) _____

OCCUPATION _____

SOMETHING ALIVE (PLURAL) _____

ANIMAL _____

VERB ENDING IN "ING" _____

TYPE OF BUILDING _____

ADJECTIVE _____

VERB _____

PLURAL NOUN _____

ANIMAL (PLURAL) _____

MAD LIBS
DIARY FROM
THE BLACK LAGOON

Dear Diary: It was another _____ day here at the lagoon. A
ADJECTIVE

couple of _____ came to swim. I thought it would
SOMETHING ALIVE (PLURAL)

be a/an _____ idea to go say "_____" and make
ADJECTIVE   SILLY WORD

friends. Of course, the moment they saw me rise out of the water

covered in _____, they screamed, "_____!
PLURAL NOUN   EXCLAMATION

It's the creature of the _____ lagoon!" and ran away. I
COLOR

can't help it if I have _____ on my cheeks and webbed
PLURAL NOUN

_____. I have feelings just like any other
PART OF THE BODY (PLURAL)

_____. I just wish _____ could see
OCCUPATION   SOMETHING ALIVE (PLURAL)

me for the lonely _____ that I really am. My only friends
ANIMAL

are the fish _____ in the lake. I wish I could live inside
VERB ENDING IN "ING"

a big _____ instead of a/an _____ lagoon like
TYPE OF BUILDING   ADJECTIVE

this one. But until I do, I'll just have to _____ with the
VERB

_____ living in here. At least they don't care that I smell
PLURAL NOUN

like _____.
ANIMAL (PLURAL)

From MONSTER MASH MAD LIBS® • Copyright © 2021 by Penguin Random House LLC

MAD LIBS® is fun to play with friends, but you can also play it by yourself! To begin with, DO NOT look at the story on the page below. Fill in the blanks on this page with the words called for. Then, using the words you have selected, fill in the blank spaces in the story.

Now you've created your own hilarious MAD LIBS® game!

BIGFOOT

ADJECTIVE _____

PART OF THE BODY (PLURAL) _____

ADJECTIVE _____

VERB ENDING IN "ING" _____

NUMBER _____

NOUN _____

SOMETHING ALIVE _____

ADJECTIVE _____

PLURAL NOUN _____

CELEBRITY _____

SOMETHING ALIVE (PLURAL) _____

ADVERB _____

ADJECTIVE _____

PART OF THE BODY _____

OCCUPATION _____

ADJECTIVE _____

A PLACE _____

PLURAL NOUN _____

MAD LIBS®

BIGFOOT

Hello. Me name is Sasquatch, but you may know me better as

_____ -foot. People call me that name because me
　　ADJECTIVE

_____ are very, very _____ . You may
PART OF THE BODY (PLURAL)　　　　　　　　　ADJECTIVE

have seen photos or videos of me _____ in the forest.
　　　　　　　　　　　　　　　VERB ENDING IN "ING"

If not, me tell you that me am _____ feet tall and me body is
　　　　　　　　　　　　NUMBER

covered in brown _____ like a/an _____ . Me
　　　　　　　NOUN　　　　　　　　　SOMETHING ALIVE

favorite food is _____ _____ . Me am like the
　　　　　ADJECTIVE　　　　PLURAL NOUN

_____ of the forest because _____
　　CELEBRITY　　　　　　　　　　SOMETHING ALIVE (PLURAL)

always trying to take picture of me to put on thing called internet. But

me always _____ run away before they can see me. Me also
　　　　ADVERB

have cousin named _____ - _____ . He just as tall
　　　　　　　ADJECTIVE　　　PART OF THE BODY

as me and look like a big, hairy _____ . We not see each other
　　　　　　　　　　　　OCCUPATION

too much because he even more _____ than me. Me hope
　　　　　　　　　　　ADJECTIVE

you come visit (the) _____ where me live and we can go scare
　　　　　　A PLACE

all the _____ together!
　　PLURAL NOUN

MAD LIBS® is fun to play with friends, but you can also play it by yourself! To begin with, DO NOT look at the story on the page below. Fill in the blanks on this page with the words called for. Then, using the words you have selected, fill in the blank spaces in the story.

Now you've created your own hilarious MAD LIBS® game!

HYDE AND DRINK

OCCUPATION _____

NOUN _____

ADJECTIVE _____

VERB _____

SOMETHING ALIVE _____

TYPE OF LIQUID _____

NOUN _____

ADJECTIVE _____

PLURAL NOUN _____

ADVERB _____

VERB _____

SILLY WORD _____

PLURAL NOUN _____

ADJECTIVE _____

PLURAL NOUN _____

NUMBER _____

ADJECTIVE _____

CELEBRITY _____

MAD LIBS®

HYDE AND DRINK

I am the world-famous _____ Dr. Jekyll! I created the
                          OCCUPATION

_____ that can turn me into the _____
          NOUN   ADJECTIVE

monster known as Mr. _____! Today, I'll teach you how
                            VERB

to make your very own potion that will turn you into a terrifying

_____ , just like me! First, you must boil _____
 SOMETHING ALIVE   TYPE OF LIQUID

inside an old _____ until it smells quite _____ .
                  NOUN   ADJECTIVE

Next, get a handful of gooey _____ and _____
                              PLURAL NOUN   ADVERB

mix them with the liquid until it starts to _____ . Lastly,
                                                VERB

take some di-oxy-_____-ide and shake it as hard as you
                    SILLY WORD

can until you see _____ start to form inside, then mix
                      PLURAL NOUN

it with the other solution. Drink it if you dare, as it will taste like

_____ _____ . Now wait _____
    ADJECTIVE   PLURAL NOUN   NUMBER

minutes, and if you followed these instructions correctly, you'll turn

into a/an _____ monster called Mr. _____!
            ADJECTIVE   CELEBRITY

MAD LIBS® is fun to play with friends, but you can also play it by yourself! To begin with, DO NOT look at the story on the page below. Fill in the blanks on this page with the words called for. Then, using the words you have selected, fill in the blank spaces in the story.

Now you've created your own hilarious MAD LIBS® game!

TROLLING FOR GOBLINS

VERB ENDING IN "ING" _____

PLURAL NOUN _____

ADJECTIVE _____

ADJECTIVE _____

NOUN _____

NUMBER _____

SOMETHING ALIVE _____

PLURAL NOUN _____

PART OF THE BODY (PLURAL) _____

VEHICLE _____

A PLACE _____

NOUN _____

ARTICLE OF CLOTHING _____

VERB _____

NOUN _____

A PLACE _____

SOMETHING ALIVE (PLURAL) _____

ADVERB _____

MAD LIBS

TROLLING FOR GOBLINS

When you're _____ through the mountains or dense
_____ VERB ENDING IN "ING"
_____ , you may encounter a troll or goblin, so it's very
PLURAL NOUN
_____ to know how to tell the difference! The first
ADJECTIVE
_____ difference you'll notice between a troll and a goblin
ADJECTIVE
is the size of the _____ . Trolls are almost _____
NOUN   NUMBER
times bigger than goblins! Trolls are said to look very similar to a/an
_____ , while goblins have green skin and wild
SOMETHING ALIVE
_____ growing atop their _____ .
PLURAL NOUN   PART OF THE BODY (PLURAL)
Trolls prefer to live under a/an _____ or under bridges,
VEHICLE
while goblins would rather live in (the) _____ . Perhaps
A PLACE
the most important difference is that a goblin will use their magical
_____ to steal your gold or _____ , whereas a
NOUN   ARTICLE OF CLOTHING
troll may try to _____ you if they're hungry! Luckily, a troll
VERB
will turn into a/an _____ if they step into the sun, so always
NOUN
make sure it's sunny before you go hiking in (the) _____ .
A PLACE
Both goblins and trolls dislike _____ , so be
SOMETHING ALIVE (PLURAL)
_____ careful if you see one!
ADVERB

From MONSTER MASH MAD LIBS® • Copyright © 2021 by Penguin Random House LLC

MAD LIBS® is fun to play with friends, but you can also play it by yourself! To begin with, DO NOT look at the story on the page below. Fill in the blanks on this page with the words called for. Then, using the words you have selected, fill in the blank spaces in the story.

Now you've created your own hilarious MAD LIBS® game!

CHEW ON THIS

SOMETHING ALIVE (PLURAL) _____

PLURAL NOUN _____

ADJECTIVE _____

VERB _____

PLURAL NOUN _____

ANIMAL _____

ADJECTIVE _____

PART OF THE BODY (PLURAL) _____

TYPE OF LIQUID _____

SOMETHING ALIVE (PLURAL) _____

SAME SOMETHING ALIVE (PLURAL) _____

TYPE OF FOOD (PLURAL) _____

NOUN _____

ANIMAL (PLURAL) _____

A PLACE _____

NOUN _____

OCCUPATION _____

MAD LIBS®

CHEW ON THIS

Do your friends have boring pets like _____ or
                                     SOMETHING ALIVE (PLURAL)

_____? If you've always wanted a/an _____-looking
PLURAL NOUN   ADJECTIVE

pet that'll make people _____ in fear, then a chupacabra is
                        VERB

perfect for you! Chupacabras are magical _____ known for
                                         PLURAL NOUN

looking like a hairless _____ with _____ skin.
                        ANIMAL   ADJECTIVE

Chupacabras have very sharp _____ that they use
                           PART OF THE BODY (PLURAL)

to suck the _____ from _____
            TYPE OF LIQUID   SOMETHING ALIVE (PLURAL)

when they're hungry. But don't worry if you don't have

_____ to feed your pet chupacabra. It'll be just
SAME SOMETHING ALIVE (PLURAL)

as happy if you let it eat a bag of _____. Chupacabras
                                   TYPE OF FOOD (PLURAL)

may not like playing normal pet games like fetch the _____,
                                                     NOUN

but they love chasing _____ around (the) _____.
                      ANIMAL (PLURAL)   A PLACE

Sure, your pet chupacabra may mess up your _____ now and
                                           NOUN

then, but that doesn't mean it won't love cuddling up with you! So have

fun with your new pet chupacabra. Just make sure it doesn't eat your

next-door _____.
          OCCUPATION

MAD LIBS® is fun to play with friends, but you can also play it by yourself! To begin with, DO NOT look at the story on the page below. Fill in the blanks on this page with the words called for. Then, using the words you have selected, fill in the blank spaces in the story.

Now you've created your own hilarious MAD LIBS® game!

OGRE AND OUT

LAST NAME _____

OCCUPATION _____

ADJECTIVE _____

EXCLAMATION _____

PLURAL NOUN _____

ADJECTIVE _____

ADJECTIVE _____

PLURAL NOUN _____

ANIMAL _____

NOUN _____

NOUN _____

ADVERB _____

SOMETHING ALIVE (PLURAL) _____

SILLY WORD _____

TYPE OF LIQUID _____

OCCUPATION _____

VERB _____

ADJECTIVE _____

MAD LIBS®

OGRE AND OUT

One day our principal, Mrs. _____ , came into our classroom
                                 LAST NAME

and told us that we'd be having a substitute _____ for the rest
                                              OCCUPATION

of the school year. We were _____ when we saw an ogre walk
                             ADJECTIVE

into the classroom. "Hello, class! My name is Mr. _____ ,"
                                                   EXCLAMATION

he growled. "But you can call me ' _____ ' for short."
                                   PLURAL NOUN

Having an ogre as a substitute was the most _____
                                             ADJECTIVE

experience of my life! He had green skin, a/an _____ head,
                                                ADJECTIVE

and two long _____ sticking out of his mouth. He smelled
              PLURAL NOUN

like a/an _____ and carried a huge wooden _____
          ANIMAL   NOUN

that he would pound on the _____ every time he
                            NOUN

_____ laughed. His favorite subjects to teach were math and
ADVERB

"How to Scare the _____ that Live in the Village."
                   SOMETHING ALIVE (PLURAL)

Every day, he would greet us by saying "Fee-Fi-Fo-_____ ,
                                                    SILLY WORD

I smell the _____ of a/an _____ !" Then he'd
             TYPE OF LIQUID   OCCUPATION

say that if he was hungry, he'd _____ any student who
                                 VERB

didn't turn in their homework. I think he was joking, but I was too

_____ to find out.
ADJECTIVE

MAD LIBS® is fun to play with friends, but you can also play it by yourself! To begin with, DO NOT look at the story on the page below. Fill in the blanks on this page with the words called for. Then, using the words you have selected, fill in the blank spaces in the story.

Now you've created your own hilarious MAD LIBS® game!

BUMP IN THE NIGHT

NOUN _____

PLURAL NOUN _____

TYPE OF BUILDING _____

VERB _____

PLURAL NOUN _____

SILLY WORD _____

PART OF THE BODY _____

NOUN _____

ANIMAL _____

NOUN _____

VERB ENDING IN "ING" _____

TYPE OF FOOD (PLURAL) _____

VERB _____

ADJECTIVE _____

TYPE OF LIQUID _____

EXCLAMATION _____

SOMETHING ALIVE _____

NOUN _____

MAD LIBS

BUMP IN THE NIGHT

Is there a creature living under your _____?
NOUN
Answer these _____ to find out if you're sharing your _____
PLURAL NOUN   TYPE OF BUILDING
with a monster!

- When you _____ at night, do you hear strange
  VERB
  _____ that sound like _____?
  PLURAL NOUN   SILLY WORD

- Have you ever seen a hairy _____ reaching out from
  PART OF THE BODY
  under your _____?
  NOUN

- Is your pet _____ afraid to come into your bedroom at
  ANIMAL
  _____-time?
  NOUN

- Do you suspect something might be _____
  VERB ENDING IN "ING"
  all the _____ in your refrigerator while you
  TYPE OF FOOD (PLURAL)
  _____?
  VERB

- Do you find puddles of _____ _____
  ADJECTIVE   TYPE OF LIQUID
  around your bedroom?

If you answered "_____" to any of these questions, you
EXCLAMATION
have a/an _____ under your _____.
SOMETHING ALIVE   NOUN

MAD LIBS® is fun to play with friends, but you can also play it by yourself! To begin with, DO NOT look at the story on the page below. Fill in the blanks on this page with the words called for. Then, using the words you have selected, fill in the blank spaces in the story.

Now you've created your own hilarious MAD LIBS® game!

GET READY TO FLEA

SOMETHING ALIVE _____

PART OF THE BODY _____

ADJECTIVE _____

ADJECTIVE _____

VERB _____

SILLY WORD _____

ANIMAL _____

ADJECTIVE _____

ANIMAL (PLURAL) _____

TYPE OF LIQUID _____

ADJECTIVE _____

PLURAL NOUN _____

TYPE OF FOOD _____

PART OF THE BODY _____

NUMBER _____

VERB ENDING IN "ING" _____

PLURAL NOUN _____

A PLACE _____

MAD LIBS®

GET READY TO FLEA

Are you a were-_____ whose _____ gets
_{SOMETHING ALIVE}   _{PART OF THE BODY}

itchy every time the moon is _____? You probably have
_{ADJECTIVE}

a/an _____ case of werewolf fleas! But there's no need to
_{ADJECTIVE}

_____ in frustration—just go out and grab a bottle of
_{VERB}

Dr. _____'s werewolf _____ remover! Made with
_{SILLY WORD}   _{ANIMAL}

the most _____ ingredients possible, our flea remover is
_{ADJECTIVE}

guaranteed to make all those itchy _____ disappear
_{ANIMAL (PLURAL)}

forever. Every bottle of flea remover contains a special blend of

_____ and _____-smelling _____ to
_{TYPE OF LIQUID}   _{ADJECTIVE}   _{PLURAL NOUN}

make your fur as smooth as a/an _____. Just pour some
_{TYPE OF FOOD}

of our flea remover on your _____ and wait _____
_{PART OF THE BODY}   _{NUMBER}

minutes. You'll be _____ with joy as you watch all
_{VERB ENDING IN "ING"}

the _____ hop off your body so they never bother you
_{PLURAL NOUN}

again! Get howling and buy our werewolf flea remover at your local

_____ now!
_{A PLACE}

MAD LIBS® is fun to play with friends, but you can also play it by yourself! To begin with, DO NOT look at the story on the page below. Fill in the blanks on this page with the words called for. Then, using the words you have selected, fill in the blank spaces in the story.

Now you've created your own hilarious MAD LIBS® game!

MONSTER BASH

PLURAL NOUN _____

ANIMAL (PLURAL) _____

NOUN _____

OCCUPATION _____

PLURAL NOUN _____

VERB _____

ADJECTIVE _____

TYPE OF LIQUID _____

ADJECTIVE _____

TYPE OF FOOD (PLURAL) _____

OCCUPATION (PLURAL) _____

ADJECTIVE _____

PART OF THE BODY (PLURAL) _____

NOUN _____

ADJECTIVE _____

VERB _____

A PLACE _____

ARTICLE OF CLOTHING (PLURAL) _____

MAD LIBS®

MONSTER BASH

Listen up, all you creepy _____ and growling
PLURAL NOUN

_____! You're invited to Dr. _____'s Mad
ANIMAL (PLURAL)   NOUN

_____ Monster Party! DJ Frankenmeyer will be in the
OCCUPATION

house spinning some awesome _____, so be ready to
PLURAL NOUN

_____ all night long on the dance floor! All that fun is sure
VERB

to make you creatures of the night hungry for some _____
ADJECTIVE

snacks, so we'll be pouring _____ for all you wannabe
TYPE OF LIQUID

vampires and serving up platters of _____ deep-fried
ADJECTIVE

_____ for trolls and _____ alike! If you
TYPE OF FOOD (PLURAL)   OCCUPATION (PLURAL)

want some _____ party games, we've got those, too. Get
ADJECTIVE

ready to bob for zombie _____ and pin the
PART OF THE BODY (PLURAL)

_____ on the werewolf! At the next _____ moon, fly,
NOUN   ADJECTIVE

creep, or _____ to the castle on top of (the) _____
VERB   A PLACE

and get ready to party until your _____ fall off!
ARTICLE OF CLOTHING (PLURAL)

From MONSTER MASH MAD LIBS® • Copyright © 2021 by Penguin Random House LLC

MAD LIBS® is fun to play with friends, but you can also play it by yourself! To begin with, DO NOT look at the story on the page below. Fill in the blanks on this page with the words called for. Then, using the words you have selected, fill in the blank spaces in the story.

Now you've created your own hilarious MAD LIBS® game!

TOO CLOSE FOR COMFORT

ADJECTIVE _____

PART OF THE BODY (PLURAL) _____

VERB _____

SOMETHING ALIVE _____

PART OF THE BODY _____

ADJECTIVE _____

NOUN _____

PART OF THE BODY _____

NOUN _____

VERB _____

ADJECTIVE _____

VERB ENDING IN "ING" _____

NUMBER _____

ADJECTIVE _____

MAD LIBS

TOO CLOSE FOR COMFORT

Gilga the Hydra is interviewed for a web series on monsters:

Interviewer: It's _____ to meet you, Gilga. Tell me,
ADJECTIVE

what are some of the challenges of being a creature with seven

_____ ?
PART OF THE BODY (PLURAL)

Head #1: When we sleep, all the other heads _____ louder
VERB

than a/an _____ and keep me awake!
SOMETHING ALIVE

Head #2: Try being the _____ next to you! Your breath
PART OF THE BODY

smells like a/an _____ _____ !
ADJECTIVE   NOUN

Head #7: Every time we eat, Head #3 chews with her _____
PART OF THE BODY

open!

Head #6: And Head #5 wants to be an internet _____ , but
NOUN

she can't even _____ !
VERB

Head #5: You're just _____ that I have a better
ADJECTIVE

_____ voice than you do!
VERB ENDING IN "ING"

Interviewer: Wow. I never knew having _____ heads could
NUMBER

be so _____ !
ADJECTIVE

MAD LIBS® is fun to play with friends, but you can also play it by yourself! To begin with, DO NOT look at the story on the page below. Fill in the blanks on this page with the words called for. Then, using the words you have selected, fill in the blank spaces in the story.

Now you've created your own hilarious MAD LIBS® game!

SCARE STYLIST

ADJECTIVE _____

OCCUPATION _____

PART OF THE BODY _____

ADJECTIVE _____

ADJECTIVE _____

CELEBRITY _____

NOUN _____

ADVERB _____

NOUN _____

PLURAL NOUN _____

VERB (PAST TENSE) _____

NOUN _____

PART OF THE BODY _____

ANIMAL _____

PLURAL NOUN _____

ADJECTIVE _____

VERB _____

NOUN _____

MAD LIBS

SCARE STYLIST

Hello, my _____ monsters, and welcome to Medusa's
        ADJECTIVE

_____ video channel. If you have snakes growing out of
    OCCUPATION

your _____ like I do, then you'll learn all the most
        PART OF THE BODY

_____ ways to style them. If you want a/an _____
    ADJECTIVE   ADJECTIVE

look like _____ , just grab a/an _____ and use
            CELEBRITY   NOUN

it to _____ comb the snakes to the left before adding
        ADVERB

_____ gel to keep your snakes in place. If you want
    NOUN

something more old-fashioned, use _____ to curl your
                                            PLURAL NOUN

snakes, and you'll look like you just _____ out of a
                                        VERB (PAST TENSE)

fashion _____! And if you're looking for something more
            NOUN

daring, use _____ spray to hold your snakes straight up
                PART OF THE BODY

in a mo-_____ style. Of course, the key to any good style
            ANIMAL

is to feed your snakes _____ to keep them looking
                            PLURAL NOUN

_____ and happy. And whatever you do, don't _____
    ADJECTIVE   VERB

at yourself in a mirror, because if you do, your snakes will turn you

into a granite _____!
                    NOUN

MAD LIBS® is fun to play with friends, but you can also play it by yourself! To begin with, DO NOT look at the story on the page below. Fill in the blanks on this page with the words called for. Then, using the words you have selected, fill in the blank spaces in the story.

Now you've created your own hilarious MAD LIBS® game!

HOW TO KNOW IF YOU'VE BEEN BITTEN BY A VAMPIRE

PART OF THE BODY _____

PLURAL NOUN _____

ADJECTIVE _____

LAST NAME _____

SOMETHING ALIVE (PLURAL) _____

TYPE OF LIQUID _____

VERB _____

NOUN _____

NOUN _____

ADVERB _____

PART OF THE BODY (PLURAL) _____

PLURAL NOUN _____

OCCUPATION (PLURAL) _____

NOUN _____

PART OF THE BODY _____

NUMBER _____

NOUN _____

MAD LIBS®
HOW TO KNOW IF YOU'VE BEEN BITTEN BY A VAMPIRE

Have you recently been bitten on the _____ by a bat?
PART OF THE BODY

Answer these _____ to find out if the _____ bat
PLURAL NOUN   ADJECTIVE

that bit you is really a vampire!

• Have you started to introduce yourself as Count _____?
LAST NAME

If so, do you have the sudden urge to bite _____
SOMETHING ALIVE (PLURAL)

and suck their _____?
TYPE OF LIQUID

• Do you _____ during the day in a wooden
VERB

_____ or do you transform into a/an _____
NOUN   NOUN

when you _____ flap your _____?
ADVERB   PART OF THE BODY (PLURAL)

• Do you only want to wear black _____?
PLURAL NOUN

• Do _____ keep trying to drive a wooden
OCCUPATION (PLURAL)

_____ into your _____?
NOUN   PART OF THE BODY

If you answered "yes" to more than _____ of these questions,
NUMBER

better get out of the sun—you just might be a/an _____!
NOUN

MAD LIBS® is fun to play with friends, but you can also play it by yourself! To begin with, DO NOT look at the story on the page below. Fill in the blanks on this page with the words called for. Then, using the words you have selected, fill in the blank spaces in the story.

Now you've created your own hilarious MAD LIBS® game!

YETI OR NOT

SILLY WORD _____

ADJECTIVE _____

NOUN _____

A PLACE _____

OCCUPATION (PLURAL) _____

NUMBER _____

NOUN _____

PART OF THE BODY _____

ADVERB _____

VERB _____

SOMETHING ALIVE _____

NOUN _____

ANIMAL _____

ADJECTIVE _____

NOUN _____

PLURAL NOUN _____

ARTICLE OF CLOTHING _____

NOUN _____

MAD LIBS®

YETI OR NOT

Welcome to Mount _____ , home to a/an _____
                     SILLY WORD   ADJECTIVE

creature known as the abominable _____ -man. It is also
                                          NOUN

known as the yeti, which translates to " _____ bear." Many
                                              A PLACE

_____ who have climbed the snow-covered mountain
OCCUPATION (PLURAL)

claim to have seen the yeti. They say the yeti stands _____
                                                          NUMBER

feet tall, is covered in white _____ , and leaves huge
                                      NOUN

_____ -prints in the snow. Yetis are _____ shy
PART OF THE BODY   ADVERB

creatures, so they'll always run and _____ when someone sees
                                          VERB

them. A yeti's favorite place to hide is behind a/an _____ .
                                                     SOMETHING ALIVE

A yeti's favorite activities are _____ -ball fights with its
                                       NOUN

_____ friends and sledding down the mountain on a/an
    ANIMAL

_____ _____ . Since the mountain is always covered
  ADJECTIVE   NOUN

in _____ , even in the summer, make sure to wear a warm
   PLURAL NOUN

_____ if you go searching for the yeti. And bring a/an
ARTICLE OF CLOTHING

_____ to take plenty of photos!
    NOUN

MAD LIBS® is fun to play with friends, but you can also play it by yourself! To begin with, DO NOT look at the story on the page below. Fill in the blanks on this page with the words called for. Then, using the words you have selected, fill in the blank spaces in the story.

Now you've created your own hilarious MAD LIBS® game!

AN EYE FOR TROUBLE

ADJECTIVE _____

PART OF THE BODY _____

NOUN _____

SAME PART OF THE BODY _____

ADJECTIVE _____

SOMETHING ALIVE (PLURAL) _____

ADJECTIVE _____

A PLACE _____

PLURAL NOUN _____

ADJECTIVE _____

VERB _____

A PLACE _____

VERB _____

OCCUPATION (PLURAL) _____

PLURAL NOUN _____

PLURAL NOUN _____

NUMBER _____

VERB ENDING IN "ING" _____

MAD LIBS

AN EYE FOR TROUBLE

Being a cyclops isn't always as _____ as it seems. The first
                                    ADJECTIVE

problem is that I only have one _____. It gets really
                                    PART OF THE BODY

difficult to see when my _____ grows too long and hangs
                              NOUN

down over my _____. But the most _____
                  SAME PART OF THE BODY   ADJECTIVE

problem I have is all the _____ living at the
                              SOMETHING ALIVE (PLURAL)

bottom of my mountain. Every month or so, they get all _____
                                                            ADJECTIVE

and come marching up to my _____ waving torches and
                                  A PLACE

_____. They shout _____ things like
        PLURAL NOUN   ADJECTIVE

"_____ the cyclops!" Usually when they storm up, I just
      VERB

stomp out of my _____ and _____ loudly a few
                      A PLACE   VERB

times. This scares most of the _____ away, but some of
                                  OCCUPATION (PLURAL)

them always try to stab me with their _____. I usually
                                          PLURAL NOUN

throw a few _____ at them to make the rest of the people
                PLURAL NOUN

run away, too. Maybe if I had _____ eyes instead of just
                                    NUMBER

one, the villagers would leave me alone, but until that day, I'll just keep

_____ them when they bother me.
    VERB ENDING IN "ING"

MAD LIBS® is fun to play with friends, but you can also play it by yourself! To begin with, DO NOT look at the story on the page below. Fill in the blanks on this page with the words called for. Then, using the words you have selected, fill in the blank spaces in the story.

Now you've created your own hilarious MAD LIBS® game!

DON'T LOSE YOUR HEAD

NOUN _____

ADJECTIVE _____

OCCUPATION _____

NOUN _____

ADJECTIVE _____

ADJECTIVE _____

PLURAL NOUN _____

NOUN _____

PART OF THE BODY _____

ADVERB _____

SOMETHING ALIVE _____

NOUN _____

SOMETHING ALIVE (PLURAL) _____

ADJECTIVE _____

ADJECTIVE _____

NOUN _____

VERB ENDING IN "ING" _____

MAD LIBS

DON'T LOSE YOUR HEAD

An interview with the Headless Horseman:

Interviewer: Welcome to "Interview with a/an _____."
                                                            NOUN
Today we'll be interviewing a/an _____ creature, the
                                      ADJECTIVE
Headless _____! Your fans are wondering, what's it like
         OCCUPATION
having a/an _____ for a head?
              NOUN

Headless Horseman: It's absolutely _____. First I had to dig
                                              ADJECTIVE
out all the _____ _____ that were inside it. Then
              ADJECTIVE   PLURAL NOUN
I used a/an _____ to carve a new _____. On dark
               NOUN   PART OF THE BODY
nights, I'll _____ ride around on my _____,
                ADVERB   SOMETHING ALIVE
take off my _____, and throw it at _____
                 NOUN   SOMETHING ALIVE (PLURAL)
to scare them!

Interviewer: Sounds _____!
                           ADJECTIVE

Headless Horseman: But the most _____ part of being the
                                          ADJECTIVE
Headless Horseman is that I never have to buy a/an _____ to
                                                        NOUN
wear when I go trick-or-_____ on Halloween!
                          VERB ENDING IN "ING"

MAD LIBS®

DAY OF THE DEAD
MAD LIBS

by Karl Jones

MAD LIBS®
INSTRUCTIONS

MAD LIBS® is a game for people who don't like games! It can be played by one, two, three, four, or forty.

● RIDICULOUSLY SIMPLE DIRECTIONS

In this tablet you will find stories containing blank spaces where words are left out. One player, the READER, selects one of these stories. The READER does not tell anyone what the story is about. Instead, he/she asks the other players, the WRITERS, to give him/her words. These words are used to fill in the blank spaces in the story.

● TO PLAY

The READER asks each WRITER in turn to call out a word—an adjective or a noun or whatever the space calls for—and uses them to fill in the blank spaces in the story. The result is a MAD LIBS® game.

When the READER then reads the completed MAD LIBS® game to the other players, they will discover that they have written a story that is fantastic, screamingly funny, shocking, silly, crazy, or just plain dumb—depending upon which words each WRITER called out.

● EXAMPLE (*Before* and *After*)

"_____!" he said _____
     EXCLAMATION   ADVERB

as he jumped into his convertible _____ and
                                            NOUN

drove off with his _____ wife.
                     ADJECTIVE

"__OUCH__!" he said __HAPPILY__
     EXCLAMATION   ADVERB

as he jumped into his convertible __CAT__ and
                                            NOUN

drove off with his __BRAVE__ wife.
                     ADJECTIVE

In case you have forgotten what adjectives, adverbs, nouns, and verbs are, here is a quick review:

An ADJECTIVE describes something or somebody. *Lumpy, soft, ugly, messy,* and *short* are adjectives.

An ADVERB tells how something is done. It modifies a verb and usually ends in "ly." *Modestly, stupidly, greedily,* and *carefully* are adverbs.

A NOUN is the name of a person, place, or thing. *Sidewalk, umbrella, bridle, bathtub,* and *nose* are nouns.

A VERB is an action word. *Run, pitch, jump,* and *swim* are verbs. Put the verbs in past tense if the directions say PAST TENSE. *Ran, pitched, jumped,* and *swam* are verbs in the past tense.

When we ask for A PLACE, we mean any sort of place: a country or city (*Spain, Cleveland*) or a room (*bathroom, kitchen*).

An EXCLAMATION or SILLY WORD is any sort of funny sound, gasp, grunt, or outcry, like *Wow!, Ouch!, Whomp!, Ick!,* and *Gadzooks!*

When we ask for specific words, like a NUMBER, a COLOR, an ANIMAL, or a PART OF THE BODY, we mean a word that is one of those things, like *seven, blue, horse,* or *head.*

When we ask for a PLURAL, it means more than one. For example, *cat* pluralized is *cats.*

MAD LIBS® is fun to play with friends, but you can also play it by yourself! To begin with, DO NOT look at the story on the page below. Fill in the blanks on this page with the words called for. Then, using the words you have selected, fill in the blank spaces in the story.

Now you've created your own hilarious MAD LIBS® game!

DAY OF THE DEAD, TRANSLATED

PLURAL NOUN _____

ADVERB _____

PART OF THE BODY _____

PLURAL NOUN _____

ADJECTIVE _____

NOUN _____

NOUN _____

VERB _____

ADJECTIVE _____

TYPE OF FOOD _____

ADJECTIVE _____

ADVERB _____

PLURAL NOUN _____

NOUN _____

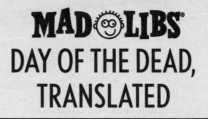

MAD LIBS®
DAY OF THE DEAD, TRANSLATED

Learn what these Spanish _____ mean in English!

PLURAL NOUN

Calavera: _____ means "skull," but during Day of the Dead, it

ADVERB

also refers to a mask worn on the _____ and a poem honoring

PART OF THE BODY

_____.

PLURAL NOUN

Papel Picado: This is a fun craft using _____ _____

ADJECTIVE   NOUN

created for Day of the Dead celebrations. It means "cut paper."

Vela: This is the _____ for "candle," often used to _____

NOUN   VERB

up an *ofrenda* (a holiday shrine) at night.

Almas: This word means "souls," what remains of the _____

ADJECTIVE

loved ones we celebrate during Day of the Dead.

Pan de Muerto: Literally "_____ of the Dead," this is

TYPE OF FOOD

_____ bread baked for the holiday.

ADJECTIVE

Flor: The word for "flower." Marigolds are _____ used to

ADVERB

decorate the *ofrendas*.

Día de los Muertos: The Spanish _____ that translate to

PLURAL NOUN

"_____ of the Dead."

NOUN

MAD LIBS® is fun to play with friends, but you can also play it by yourself! To begin with, DO NOT look at the story on the page below. Fill in the blanks on this page with the words called for. Then, using the words you have selected, fill in the blank spaces in the story.

Now you've created your own hilarious MAD LIBS® game!

NOT-SO-TRADITIONAL
PAN DE MUERTO RECIPE

TYPE OF FOOD _____

ADJECTIVE _____

SAME TYPE OF FOOD _____

TYPE OF LIQUID _____

NOUN _____

NOUN _____

ADJECTIVE _____

VERB ENDING IN "ING" _____

ADJECTIVE _____

ADVERB _____

VERB _____

ADJECTIVE _____

VERB _____

NOUN _____

NOUN _____

VERB _____

MAD LIBS®
NOT-SO-TRADITIONAL
PAN DE MUERTO RECIPE

Heat milk and _____ together in a/an _____
                 TYPE OF FOOD   ADJECTIVE

saucepan, until the _____ melts. Remove from the
                       SAME TYPE OF FOOD

heat and add warm _____. In a large _____,
                       TYPE OF LIQUID   NOUN

combine flour, yeast, salt, _____-seed, and sugar. Beat in the
                                NOUN

_____ milk mixture, then add eggs and beat some more. Stir
  ADJECTIVE

in flour one spoonful at a time and continue _____
                                                VERB ENDING IN "ING"

until the dough is _____. Turn the dough out onto a/an
                       ADJECTIVE

_____ floured surface and _____ until smooth. Let
  ADVERB   VERB

the dough rise in a/an _____ place until it doubles in size.
                           ADJECTIVE

Punch the dough down and _____ it into a large round loaf.
                             VERB

Place dough on a baking _____, loosely cover with plastic
                            NOUN

wrap, and let it rise in a warm place until it doubles in size. Bake at

350°F for about 35 to 45 minutes. Remove from _____ and
                                                    NOUN

let cool. Then _____ and enjoy!
                   VERB

MAD LIBS® is fun to play with friends, but you can also play it by yourself! To begin with, DO NOT look at the story on the page below. Fill in the blanks on this page with the words called for. Then, using the words you have selected, fill in the blank spaces in the story.

Now you've created your own hilarious MAD LIBS® game!

SUGAR SKULL DREAMS

VERB ENDING IN "ING" _____

NOUN _____

ADJECTIVE _____

TYPE OF LIQUID _____

PLURAL NOUN _____

TYPE OF FOOD _____

ADVERB _____

PLURAL NOUN _____

ADJECTIVE _____

VERB ENDING IN "ING" _____

NUMBER _____

TYPE OF FOOD (PLURAL) _____

ADVERB _____

PLURAL NOUN _____

VERB ENDING IN "ING" _____

EXCLAMATION _____

MAD LIBS®

SUGAR SKULL DREAMS

After _____ and decorating sugar skulls all day for
        VERB ENDING IN "ING"

your _____ of the Dead celebration, you go to sleep that
        NOUN

night and have a very _____ dream. You wake up and decide
                        ADJECTIVE

to have a glass of _____ to help you fall back to sleep. As
                    TYPE OF LIQUID

you try to remember the _____ of your dream, a vision of
                        PLURAL NOUN

_____ skulls comes clearly to your mind. You were walking
TYPE OF FOOD

_____ through the cafeteria at school. You were excited to
ADVERB

be making sugar skulls to help your deceased _____ visit
                                            PLURAL NOUN

during Day of the Dead. You heard a/an _____ noise behind
                                        ADJECTIVE

you, and after _____ around, you were confronted by
                VERB ENDING IN "ING"

_____ _____ floating toward you, dancing
NUMBER   TYPE OF FOOD (PLURAL)

a beautiful dance. You started dancing with them _____
                                                    ADVERB

and noticed that your teachers and _____ were dancing
                                    PLURAL NOUN

with you as well! Everyone was laughing, _____,
                                          VERB ENDING IN "ING"

and clapping, having a wonderful time. You didn't want it to end, but

then . . . _____! You woke up!
            EXCLAMATION

MAD LIBS® is fun to play with friends, but you can also play it by yourself! To begin with, DO NOT look at the story on the page below. Fill in the blanks on this page with the words called for. Then, using the words you have selected, fill in the blank spaces in the story.

Now you've created your own hilarious MAD LIBS® game!

AN EPITAPH ON A GRAVESTONE

NUMBER _____

VERB (PAST TENSE) _____

PERSON IN ROOM _____

VERB ENDING IN "ING" _____

ADJECTIVE _____

PLURAL NOUN _____

CELEBRITY _____

PLURAL NOUN _____

PLURAL NOUN _____

ADJECTIVE _____

PLURAL NOUN _____

PLURAL NOUN _____

NOUN _____

CELEBRITY _____

MAD LIBS®
AN EPITAPH ON A GRAVESTONE

Born: November _____, 1977
<u>NUMBER</u>

_____: April 1, 2051
<u>VERB (PAST TENSE)</u>

Here lies _____, grandparent to three _____
<u>PERSON IN ROOM</u>   <u>VERB ENDING IN "ING"</u>

granddaughters, parent to two _____ _____, and
<u>ADJECTIVE</u>   <u>PLURAL NOUN</u>

devoted spouse to _____. With courage and _____,
<u>CELEBRITY</u>   <u>PLURAL NOUN</u>

they lived life as an example of _____ and _____
<u>PLURAL NOUN</u>   <u>ADJECTIVE</u>

moral character. In times of trouble, they brought comfort and

_____ to those in need, and in times of joy, they were the
<u>PLURAL NOUN</u>

embodiment of _____.
<u>PLURAL NOUN</u>

"Be the _____ you want to see in the world."
<u>NOUN</u>

— _____
<u>CELEBRITY</u>

MAD LIBS® is fun to play with friends, but you can also play it by yourself! To begin with, DO NOT look at the story on the page below. Fill in the blanks on this page with the words called for. Then, using the words you have selected, fill in the blank spaces in the story.

Now you've created your own hilarious MAD LIBS® game!

ONE WAY TO BUILD AN OFRENDA

ADJECTIVE _____

NOUN _____

ADJECTIVE _____

TYPE OF LIQUID _____

NUMBER _____

PLURAL NOUN _____

ADJECTIVE _____

PLURAL NOUN _____

ADJECTIVE _____

ADJECTIVE _____

ADJECTIVE _____

TYPE OF FOOD _____

TYPE OF FOOD _____

PLURAL NOUN _____

MAD LIBS®
ONE WAY TO BUILD
AN OFRENDA

Creating your first *ofrenda* takes some _____ work and
_____ADJECTIVE_____

preparation. To begin, place a table against the _____. Cover
_____NOUN

the table with a/an _____ piece of fabric. Include any or all of
_____ADJECTIVE

the following items on your *ofrenda*:

- Glass of _____
  ____TYPE OF LIQUID

- Candles. Use at least _____ for each person being honored.
  _____NUMBER

- Fruits and _____. Use fresh, _____, or plastic
  ____PLURAL NOUN_____ADJECTIVE

  fruits—they all work!

- *Papel picado* banners. You can learn how to make your own

  _____ with the craft activity inside this _____ book!
  ___PLURAL NOUN_____ADJECTIVE

- *Copal* or an incense that smells _____
  _____ADJECTIVE

- Marigolds (fresh, dried, paper, or _____) or other orange,
  _____ADJECTIVE

  yellow, and magenta flowers

- *Pan de Muerto* (_____ of the Dead)
  _____TYPE OF FOOD

- Framed photograph of the person being honored

- _____ skulls
  ___TYPE OF FOOD

- Skeletons made of papier-mâché or _____
  _____PLURAL NOUN

MAD LIBS® is fun to play with friends, but you can also play it by yourself! To begin with, DO NOT look at the story on the page below. Fill in the blanks on this page with the words called for. Then, using the words you have selected, fill in the blank spaces in the story.

Now you've created your own hilarious MAD LIBS® game!

FLORIST'S PHONE ORDER SCRIPT

VERB ENDING IN "ING" _____

NOUN _____

ADVERB _____

ADJECTIVE _____

VERB (PAST TENSE) _____

NOUN _____

PLURAL NOUN _____

VERB ENDING IN "ING" _____

PLURAL NOUN _____

COLOR _____

NUMBER _____

NOUN _____

ADJECTIVE _____

VERB _____

VERB ENDING IN "ING" _____

MAD LIBS®
FLORIST'S PHONE
ORDER SCRIPT

(*Remember to smile while talking.*) Thank you for _____
VERB ENDING IN "ING"

_____ Flowers and More. Please state your name and telephone
NOUN

number _____. Also please tell us where your _____
ADVERB   ADJECTIVE

flower order needs to be _____. Will you be paying
VERB (PAST TENSE)

with _____ or credit? How many _____ will you
NOUN   PLURAL NOUN

be _____ from us? What type of _____
VERB ENDING IN "ING"   PLURAL NOUN

would you like to order? We have yellow and _____ marigolds
COLOR

available. The price is _____ dollars for each _____ of
NUMBER   NOUN

flowers. Your _____ order will be ready to _____
ADJECTIVE   VERB

tomorrow afternoon. Thank you for _____!
VERB ENDING IN "ING"

MAD LIBS® is fun to play with friends, but you can also play it by yourself! To begin with, DO NOT look at the story on the page below. Fill in the blanks on this page with the words called for. Then, using the words you have selected, fill in the blank spaces in the story.

Now you've created your own hilarious MAD LIBS® game!

DAY OF THE DEAD MAKEUP

PERSON IN ROOM _____

NUMBER _____

PLURAL NOUN _____

ADJECTIVE _____

PLURAL NOUN _____

PART OF THE BODY _____

ADJECTIVE _____

NOUN _____

ADVERB _____

PART OF THE BODY _____

COLOR _____

NOUN _____

PART OF THE BODY _____

NOUN _____

PART OF THE BODY (PLURAL) _____

ADJECTIVE _____

PLURAL NOUN _____

MAD LIBS®

DAY OF THE DEAD MAKEUP

_____ is known for their awesome makeup tutorials.
PERSON IN ROOM

_____ people view their helpful _____ daily to learn
NUMBER   PLURAL NOUN

more about the art of makeup. Watch this _____ video to learn
ADJECTIVE

how to use _____ to make your _____ look like an
PLURAL NOUN   PART OF THE BODY

authentic _calavera_:

"To achieve a/an _____ Day of the Dead _calavera_ look,
ADJECTIVE

start by buying the right supplies at your local _____
NOUN

store. Be sure to buy makeup that's made _____ for the
ADVERB

_____. You will definitely want white and black, but also get
PART OF THE BODY

_____ and green, as well as golden yellow, the color of the
COLOR

marigold _____. First, wash and dry your _____.
NOUN   PART OF THE BODY

Then apply the white _____ all over your face. Next, make
NOUN

circles with the black makeup around your _____.
PART OF THE BODY (PLURAL)

You can also use the black and white makeup to create creepy seams

or pronounced teeth so you truly look _____. Finally, use the
ADJECTIVE

other colors to make patterns and _____ that will accent
PLURAL NOUN

your look!"

MAD LIBS® is fun to play with friends, but you can also play it by yourself! To begin with, DO NOT look at the story on the page below. Fill in the blanks on this page with the words called for. Then, using the words you have selected, fill in the blank spaces in the story.

Now you've created your own hilarious MAD LIBS® game!

INVITATION TO A DAY OF THE DEAD CELEBRATION

VERB (PAST TENSE) _____

NOUN _____

ADJECTIVE _____

NOUN _____

NUMBER _____

TYPE OF FOOD _____

NOUN _____

PLURAL NOUN _____

TYPE OF FOOD _____

TYPE OF LIQUID _____

ADJECTIVE _____

NOUN _____

MAD LIBS
INVITATION TO A DAY OF THE DEAD CELEBRATION

To all our friends and _____ ones—we hope that you

VERB (PAST TENSE)

can join us for our annual _____ of the Dead Celebration!

NOUN

Who: You, our _____ friends and family!

ADJECTIVE

Where: 18 Mariposa Lane, New _____ City

NOUN

When: November _____, from 12:00 p.m. until we run out of

NUMBER

_____

TYPE OF FOOD

What: Music from a mariachi _____, poetry _____,

NOUN   PLURAL NOUN

and plenty of _____ and _____!

TYPE OF FOOD   TYPE OF LIQUID

Why: To honor our _____ ones and to celebrate our

ADJECTIVE

_____ together!

NOUN

MAD LIBS® is fun to play with friends, but you can also play it by yourself! To begin with, DO NOT look at the story on the page below. Fill in the blanks on this page with the words called for. Then, using the words you have selected, fill in the blank spaces in the story.

Now you've created your own hilarious MAD LIBS® game!

A BRIEF HISTORY OF THE AZTECS

PLURAL NOUN _____

PLURAL NOUN _____

PLURAL NOUN _____

A PLACE _____

ADJECTIVE _____

A PLACE _____

NUMBER _____

ADJECTIVE _____

TYPE OF LIQUID _____

PLURAL NOUN _____

PLURAL NOUN _____

PLURAL NOUN _____

A PLACE _____

MAD LIBS
A BRIEF HISTORY OF
THE AZTECS

Day of the _____ is a celebration of rituals and _____

PLURAL NOUN · PLURAL NOUN

taken from the Aztecs that have been blended with _____ and

PLURAL NOUN

beliefs of the Spanish colonists who came from (the) _____.

A PLACE

The Aztecs were a powerful _____ farming society that lived

ADJECTIVE

in Central _____ for _____ years before the arrival

A PLACE · NUMBER

of the conquistadors. Their capital city, Tenochtitlan, had many

_____ temples and was surrounded by _____.

ADJECTIVE · TYPE OF LIQUID

The Aztecs originally honored their _____ in July and

PLURAL NOUN

August, but the Spanish changed the date of the celebration to

November 1 and 2 to coincide with All _____' Day. Now

PLURAL NOUN

the holiday, started by these powerful _____, takes place

PLURAL NOUN

not only in (the) _____ but all over the world.

A PLACE

MAD LIBS® is fun to play with friends, but you can also play it by yourself! To begin with, DO NOT look at the story on the page below. Fill in the blanks on this page with the words called for. Then, using the words you have selected, fill in the blank spaces in the story.

Now you've created your own hilarious MAD LIBS® game!

A STORY ABOUT GREAT-GREAT-GRANDMOTHER

ADJECTIVE _____

A PLACE _____

NOUN _____

VERB (PAST TENSE) _____

PLURAL NOUN _____

PLURAL NOUN _____

VERB ENDING IN "ING" _____

VERB _____

ANIMAL (PLURAL) _____

A PLACE _____

COLOR _____

TYPE OF LIQUID _____

PART OF THE BODY (PLURAL) _____

VERB ENDING IN "ING" _____

NOUN _____

MAD LIBS
A STORY ABOUT GREAT-GREAT-GRANDMOTHER

To honor the dead, we tell stories of their lives. This is a/an

_____ story about your great-great-grandmother:
  ADJECTIVE

When Great-Great-Grandmother was young, she came to (the)

_____ with her mother and _____ to live on a
  A PLACE   NOUN

farm. A boy who _____ on the farm next door raised
                    VERB (PAST TENSE)

lots of _____ with his family, including pigs, horses, and
      PLURAL NOUN

_____. One day, the boy noticed her _____
  PLURAL NOUN   VERB ENDING IN "ING"

at his favorite horse. He asked her if she knew how to _____.
                                                  VERB

She said yes, so they borrowed a couple of _____ and
                                         ANIMAL (PLURAL)

went for a long ride around (the) _____. She noticed how the
                                  A PLACE

_____ _____ in the small stream that separated
  COLOR   TYPE OF LIQUID

their farms matched the color of his _____. After
                                PART OF THE BODY (PLURAL)

that, they went _____ together every day. And that's
                VERB ENDING IN "ING"

how Great-Great-Grandmother met Great-Great-Grand-_____!
                                                         NOUN

MAD LIBS® is fun to play with friends, but you can also play it by yourself! To begin with, DO NOT look at the story on the page below. Fill in the blanks on this page with the words called for. Then, using the words you have selected, fill in the blank spaces in the story.

Now you've created your own hilarious MAD LIBS® game!

A STORY ABOUT GREAT-GRANDFATHER

A PLACE _____

ADJECTIVE _____

VERB ENDING IN "ING" _____

ADJECTIVE _____

TYPE OF FOOD (PLURAL) _____

TYPE OF FOOD (PLURAL) _____

NUMBER _____

VERB ENDING IN "ING" _____

PLURAL NOUN _____

PLURAL NOUN _____

ADJECTIVE _____

A PLACE _____

VERB (PAST TENSE) _____

NOUN _____

MAD LIBS
A STORY ABOUT GREAT-GRANDFATHER

My great-grandfather was born and raised in (the) _____, a/an
A PLACE

_____ country where the sun was always _____.
ADJECTIVE   _VERB ENDING IN "ING"_

He grew up surrounded by _____ trees and spent
ADJECTIVE

the days of his youth climbing and playing amongst the limes,

_____, and _____ that the trees
TYPE OF FOOD (PLURAL)   _TYPE OF FOOD (PLURAL)_

produced. When he was _____ years old, his parents sent
NUMBER

him away to _____ school. At school, he missed his
VERB ENDING IN "ING"

_____ terribly and sent them many _____.
PLURAL NOUN   _PLURAL NOUN_

He spent many _____ hours by himself imagining that he
ADJECTIVE

was back in (the) _____. When he finally returned home,
A PLACE

he discovered that not much had _____. And he was
VERB (PAST TENSE)

especially happy to see his beloved _____ trees!
NOUN

MAD LIBS® is fun to play with friends, but you can also play it by yourself! To begin with, DO NOT look at the story on the page below. Fill in the blanks on this page with the words called for. Then, using the words you have selected, fill in the blank spaces in the story.

Now you've created your own hilarious MAD LIBS® game!

MAKE *PAPEL PICADO* FOR YOUR CELEBRATION!

PLURAL NOUN _____

ADJECTIVE _____

NOUN _____

NOUN _____

VERB ENDING IN "ING" _____

ADJECTIVE _____

ADJECTIVE _____

NOUN _____

NOUN _____

ADJECTIVE _____

VERB (PAST TENSE) _____

ADVERB _____

VERB ENDING IN "ING" _____

NOUN _____

VERB _____

ADJECTIVE _____

MAD LIBS®
MAKE PAPEL PICADO
FOR YOUR CELEBRATION!

Use the _____ below to create _____ *papel picado*
       PLURAL NOUN   ADJECTIVE

(cut paper) for your _____ of the Dead celebration:
                      NOUN

- Colored tissue _____, cut into 8-inch by 8-inch squares
                  NOUN

- _____ shears
    VERB ENDING IN "ING"

- A/An _____ piece of string
        ADJECTIVE

- _____ tape
    ADJECTIVE

Fold a piece of _____ paper in half from edge to _____.
              NOUN   NOUN

Cut _____ shapes in the paper, being careful that no corners
     ADJECTIVE

are _____. Unfold the tissue paper _____.
    VERB (PAST TENSE)   ADVERB

Decorate the edges by _____ zigzags or fringe. Fold
                  VERB ENDING IN "ING"

the top of the _____ (about 1/2 inch) over a long piece of
              NOUN

string and _____ it into place. Use a few sheets of tissue paper
         VERB

to make a long _____ streamer.
         ADJECTIVE

MAD LIBS® is fun to play with friends, but you can also play it by yourself! To begin with, DO NOT look at the story on the page below. Fill in the blanks on this page with the words called for. Then, using the words you have selected, fill in the blank spaces in the story.

Now you've created your own hilarious MAD LIBS® game!

ONLINE REVIEW FOR A LOCAL MEXICAN BAKERY

ADVERB _____

NOUN _____

NOUN _____

ADJECTIVE _____

PERSON IN ROOM _____

VERB ENDING IN "ING" _____

NOUN _____

TYPE OF FOOD _____

CELEBRITY _____

ADJECTIVE _____

ADJECTIVE _____

ADVERB _____

VERB ENDING IN "ING" _____

NOUN _____

SILLY WORD _____

MAD LIBS®
ONLINE REVIEW FOR A LOCAL MEXICAN BAKERY

I don't _____ leave reviews on this web-_____,
      ADVERB   NOUN

but I just had to give props to my fav new Mexican cake shop on

_____ Street!! It is literally the most _____ place I've
   NOUN   ADJECTIVE

been to since moving here from Tucson!!! First off, _____
                                              PERSON IN ROOM

was soooooooooo helpful on the phone before I ended up

_____ the bakery. My super-cute niece was having a
VERB ENDING IN "ING"

Day of the _____—themed birthday party and wanted a cake
                NOUN

decorated with _____ skulls. The folks at _____'s
           TYPE OF FOOD   CELEBRITY

Cake Shop said, "No problem!!!!!" And the cake tasted _____!
                                              ADJECTIVE

At the party, everyone was talking about how _____ it was and
                                       ADJECTIVE

asking where I had gotten it. And my niece _____ loved the
                                        ADVERB

cake design!!! I will def be _____ all my friends, and
                           VERB ENDING IN "ING"

I can't wait to order another delicious (and beautiful) _____
                                                   NOUN

from them soon!!!!!!!! _____!!!
                   SILLY WORD

MAD LIBS® is fun to play with friends, but you can also play it by yourself! To begin with, DO NOT look at the story on the page below. Fill in the blanks on this page with the words called for. Then, using the words you have selected, fill in the blank spaces in the story.

Now you've created your own hilarious MAD LIBS® game!

TO THE VISITING DEAD PERSON

PERSON IN ROOM _____

ADVERB _____

NOUN _____

ADJECTIVE _____

CELEBRITY _____

CELEBRITY _____

NUMBER _____

VERB ENDING IN "ING" _____

ADJECTIVE _____

ADJECTIVE _____

NOUN _____

NOUN _____

PLURAL NOUN _____

ADJECTIVE _____

ADJECTIVE _____

MAD LIBS®
TO THE VISITING DEAD PERSON

Dear _____,
<u>PERSON IN ROOM</u>

I miss you _____, but I'm excited that we can spend time
<u>ADVERB</u>

together during the _____ of the Dead. Want to hear
<u>NOUN</u>

some _____ news about my life? I became friends with
<u>ADJECTIVE</u>

_____ and _____. Can you believe it? The three
<u>CELEBRITY</u>   <u>CELEBRITY</u>

of us recently spent _____ days together, _____
<u>NUMBER</u>   <u>VERB ENDING IN "ING"</u>

around the country. We visited all the _____ sights, like
<u>ADJECTIVE</u>

the _____ Canyon, Mount Rushmore, the Statue of
<u>ADJECTIVE</u>

_____, the Mississippi _____, and the Rocky
<u>NOUN</u>   <u>NOUN</u>

_____. I wish you could have been there with us, but I'm so
<u>PLURAL NOUN</u>

thankful we get to see each other during this very _____ day!
<u>ADJECTIVE</u>

Who knows what _____ news I will have to report next year?
<u>ADJECTIVE</u>

Until then,

Me

MAD LIBS® is fun to play with friends, but you can also play it by yourself! To begin with, DO NOT look at the story on the page below. Fill in the blanks on this page with the words called for. Then, using the words you have selected, fill in the blank spaces in the story.

Now you've created your own hilarious MAD LIBS® game!

A TO-DO LIST

PLURAL NOUN _____

VERB ENDING IN "ING" _____

TYPE OF FOOD _____

TYPE OF LIQUID _____

PLURAL NOUN _____

NOUN _____

PLURAL NOUN _____

ADJECTIVE _____

ADJECTIVE _____

A PLACE _____

PLURAL NOUN _____

PLURAL NOUN _____

PLURAL NOUN _____

VERB ENDING IN "ING" _____

A TO-DO LIST

Before we honor our departed _____ and family, we have
PLURAL NOUN

to prepare for their return to the land of the _____.
VERB ENDING IN "ING"

Here's what we have to do:

- Make traditional _____ and _____ for
TYPE OF FOOD   TYPE OF LIQUID

  the celebration.

- Gather marigold _____ and make *papel picado*, a
PLURAL NOUN

  type of cut _____, to decorate our homes.
NOUN

- Find photographs of our loved _____ to place on
PLURAL NOUN

  our *ofrenda*.

- Gather with our family to tell _____ stories about our
ADJECTIVE

  _____ ancestors.
ADJECTIVE

- Walk the streets of (the) _____ as part of a Day of the
A PLACE

  _____ parade.
PLURAL NOUN

- Visit the cemetery to see the _____ where our
PLURAL NOUN

  _____ are buried.
PLURAL NOUN

- Celebrate our family that is still _____ and tell
VERB ENDING IN "ING"

  them that we love them.

From DAY OF THE DEAD MAD LIBS® • Copyright © 2017 by Penguin Random House LLC

MAD LIBS® is fun to play with friends, but you can also play it by yourself! To begin with, DO NOT look at the story on the page below. Fill in the blanks on this page with the words called for. Then, using the words you have selected, fill in the blank spaces in the story.

Now you've created your own hilarious MAD LIBS® game!

DAY OF THE DEAD OR HALLOWEEN?

ADVERB _____

NOUN _____

PLURAL NOUN _____

TYPE OF FOOD _____

PART OF THE BODY (PLURAL) _____

PLURAL NOUN _____

PLURAL NOUN _____

A PLACE _____

A PLACE _____

PLURAL NOUN _____

PERSON IN ROOM _____

NOUN _____

PLURAL NOUN _____

ADVERB _____

VERB _____

MAD LIBS®
DAY OF THE DEAD OR HALLOWEEN?

Day of the Dead and Halloween occur around the same time of year.

Do you know how each holiday is celebrated? Let's find out!

1. This holiday is _____ celebrated with an *ofrenda*, a

ADVERB

   handmade _____ for the dead. (DOTD)

NOUN

2. Children dress up in _____ and walk around begging

PLURAL NOUN

   for _____ during this holiday. (Halloween)

TYPE OF FOOD

3. Celebrants of this holiday paint their _____

PART OF THE BODY (PLURAL)

   with _____ to look like _____. (DOTD)

PLURAL NOUN   PLURAL NOUN

4. Primarily celebrated in (the) _____ and Latin

A PLACE

   _____, this celebration is becoming more common in

A PLACE

   the United _____ of America. (DOTD)

PLURAL NOUN

5. Decorations for this holiday can feature _____

PERSON IN ROOM

   -o'-lanterns, _____ webs, and spooky ghosts and

NOUN

   _____. (Halloween)

PLURAL NOUN

6. When begging for candy on this holiday, children _____ say,

ADVERB

   "_____ or treat." (Halloween)

VERB

Count up your score to see how you did!

From DAY OF THE DEAD MAD LIBS® • Copyright © 2017 by Penguin Random House LLC

MAD LIBS® is fun to play with friends, but you can also play it by yourself! To begin with, DO NOT look at the story on the page below. Fill in the blanks on this page with the words called for. Then, using the words you have selected, fill in the blank spaces in the story.

Now you've created your own hilarious MAD LIBS® game!

THE MONARCH MIGRATION

PLURAL NOUN _____

ADJECTIVE _____

NOUN _____

NOUN _____

ADJECTIVE _____

ADJECTIVE _____

NOUN _____

NUMBER _____

NOUN _____

ADVERB _____

ADJECTIVE _____

NOUN _____

ADJECTIVE _____

PLURAL NOUN _____

MAD LIBS®

THE MONARCH MIGRATION

The migration of monarch butterflies from the United _____

PLURAL NOUN

and Canada to Mexico is a/an _____ part of _____

ADJECTIVE   NOUN

of the Dead celebrations. Returning in early November, the

_____-flies are a symbol of the souls of _____

NOUN   ADJECTIVE

ancestors visiting the land of the living during Day of the Dead.

A/An _____ fact about the _____ migration

ADJECTIVE   NOUN

is that no single butterfly lives through the entire yearly cycle of

migration. In fact, _____ generations of butterflies participate

NUMBER

in the _____. When they _____ reach Mexico, they

NOUN   ADVERB

congregate in _____ flocks on special _____ trees.

ADJECTIVE   NOUN

A/An _____ sight, these _____ are a beautiful

ADJECTIVE   PLURAL NOUN

symbol of our relationship with the natural world.

MAD LIBS® is fun to play with friends, but you can also play it by yourself! To begin with, DO NOT look at the story on the page below. Fill in the blanks on this page with the words called for. Then, using the words you have selected, fill in the blank spaces in the story.

Now you've created your own hilarious MAD LIBS® game!

A DAY OF THE DEAD POEM

PLURAL NOUN _____

PLURAL NOUN _____

ADVERB _____

NOUN _____

PART OF THE BODY (PLURAL) _____

PLURAL NOUN _____

NOUN _____

NOUN _____

ADJECTIVE _____

NOUN _____

VERB (PAST TENSE) _____

ADJECTIVE _____

NUMBER _____

VERB (PAST TENSE) _____

NOUN _____

MAD LIBS®

A DAY OF THE DEAD POEM

To our family and _____ who are no longer with us,
    PLURAL NOUN

we send you our hopes, our _____, and our wishes.
    PLURAL NOUN

We think of you _____, remember your stories,
    ADVERB

with _____ and with joy, we recount your glories.
    NOUN

In our _____ and minds with us you'll remain,
    PART OF THE BODY (PLURAL)

till Day of the _____ when we're with you again.
    PLURAL NOUN

With glasses of water and fresh _____ *de Muerto*,
    NOUN

we offer you comfort and _____ where you're led to.
    NOUN

We built an *ofrenda*, a/an _____ shrine to remember
    ADJECTIVE

the _____ and the stories that we _____ together.
    NOUN   VERB (PAST TENSE)

It's Day of the Dead and we're _____ you're here,
    ADJECTIVE

though we wish it were more than _____ times a year.
    NUMBER

So know that you're _____ as we always remember
    VERB (PAST TENSE)

to celebrate _____ these first days in November.
    NOUN

MAD LIBS® is fun to play with friends, but you can also play it by yourself! To begin with, DO NOT look at the story on the page below. Fill in the blanks on this page with the words called for. Then, using the words you have selected, fill in the blank spaces in the story.

Now you've created your own hilarious MAD LIBS® game!

CANDLE STORE ADVERTISEMENT

ADJECTIVE _____

PLURAL NOUN _____

A PLACE _____

PERSON IN ROOM _____

NOUN _____

NOUN _____

ADJECTIVE _____

ADJECTIVE _____

NOUN _____

PLURAL NOUN _____

PART OF THE BODY _____

NOUN _____

ANIMAL _____

VERB ENDING IN "ING" _____

NOUN _____

NOUN _____

MAD LIBS®
CANDLE STORE
ADVERTISEMENT

Are you searching for a/an _____ selection of _____
ADJECTIVE   PLURAL NOUN

to light on your *ofrenda* or bring to (the) _____ during Day of
A PLACE

the Dead? Look no further than _____'s Candle Emporium,
PERSON IN ROOM

just south of _____ Road on Highway 10. We've got thousands
NOUN

of _____ varieties that will provide _____ lighting
NOUN   ADJECTIVE

for all your traditional celebratory needs. In fact, we've got the most

_____ candles you can find this side of the _____
ADJECTIVE   NOUN

River! Our _____ are famous for a very specific reason.
PLURAL NOUN

They are _____-crafted with organic _____-wax
PART OF THE BODY   NOUN

sourced from local _____ farmers. Not only will your candles
ANIMAL

add elegance to your celebration, you'll be _____ the
VERB ENDING IN "ING"

local economy. And if you're not satisfied with your order, we offer

a/an _____-back guarantee on all products sold. Follow the
NOUN

wick to the best _____ store in town!
NOUN

MAD LIBS® is fun to play with friends, but you can also play it by yourself! To begin with, DO NOT look at the story on the page below. Fill in the blanks on this page with the words called for. Then, using the words you have selected, fill in the blank spaces in the story.

Now you've created your own hilarious MAD LIBS® game!

A LETTER TO PARENTS AND STUDENTS

PLURAL NOUN _____

VERB ENDING IN "ING" _____

NOUN _____

NOUN _____

ADJECTIVE _____

VERB ENDING IN "ING" _____

NOUN _____

TYPE OF FOOD _____

ADVERB _____

PART OF THE BODY _____

NOUN _____

NOUN _____

NUMBER _____

PLURAL NOUN _____

ADJECTIVE _____

MAD☺LIBS®
A LETTER TO PARENTS AND STUDENTS

Dear _____ and students,
      PLURAL NOUN

As many of you know, this Friday we will be _____
                                         VERB ENDING IN "ING"

Day of the _____ at Stoney _____ Elementary
           NOUN   NOUN

School. I know that our hardworking students are excited about the

_____ events planned for the day. Here's how you can get
ADJECTIVE

involved. First, help your child dress up as their favorite ancestor,

_____ or dead. They will be given the chance to talk
VERB ENDING IN "ING"

about their _____ in front of their class. At lunch, students
          NOUN

will have the chance to enjoy traditional Mexican _____, as
                                     TYPE OF FOOD

well as *Pan de Muerto* _____ provided by Mrs. Martinez's
                         ADVERB

bakery. After lunch, students can enjoy _____-painting with
                                PART OF THE BODY

our _____ teacher, Mrs. D'Amore. At the end of the day, we
    NOUN

will be screening an animated Day of the _____ movie. It is
                               NOUN

rated PG-_____, so please be sure students have turned in their
       NUMBER

permission _____ so they can attend. After all, no one—
        PLURAL NOUN

living or _____!—wants to be left out of our celebration.
      ADJECTIVE

Sincerely, Principal Jones

MAD LIBS® is fun to play with friends, but you can also play it by yourself! To begin with, DO NOT look at the story on the page below. Fill in the blanks on this page with the words called for. Then, using the words you have selected, fill in the blank spaces in the story.

Now you've created your own hilarious MAD LIBS® game!

CALAVERA MASK TUTORIAL

NOUN _____

NOUN _____

PLURAL NOUN _____

ADVERB _____

PART OF THE BODY _____

PART OF THE BODY _____

PLURAL NOUN _____

PLURAL NOUN _____

PART OF THE BODY _____

ADJECTIVE _____

PLURAL NOUN _____

PLURAL NOUN _____

NOUN _____

VERB ENDING IN "ING" _____

PART OF THE BODY _____

PLURAL NOUN _____

MAD LIBS®
CALAVERA MASK TUTORIAL

What you'll need:

- One _____ of white paper
  NOUN

- A/An _____ of scissors
  NOUN

- A set of colored markers or _____
  PLURAL NOUN

- A piece of string or twine that will fit _____ around the
  ADVERB
  _____
  PART OF THE BODY

First, sketch a/an _____-shaped circle on a piece of paper.
PART OF THE BODY

Be sure to include two eye _____ and a hole for the
PLURAL NOUN

mouth. Then use your _____ to cut along the lines of
PLURAL NOUN

your sketch, including the mouth and _____holes. Decorate
PART OF THE BODY

your mask with _____ Day of the Dead designs, like flowers
ADJECTIVE

and _____. Use plenty of color! Use black to create large
PLURAL NOUN

_____around the eyes and to draw a/an _____on
PLURAL NOUN   NOUN

the forehead. Once you're finished _____ your mask,
VERB ENDING IN "ING"

use string to secure it around your _____. Then see if you can
PART OF THE BODY

make a mask for all the _____of your family!
PLURAL NOUN

From DAY OF THE DEAD MAD LIBS® • Copyright © 2017 by Penguin Random House LLC

MAD LIBS®

TRICK OR TREAT
MAD LIBS

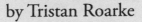

by Tristan Roarke

MAD◉LIBS®

INSTRUCTIONS

MAD LIBS® is a game for people who don't like games! It can be played by one, two, three, four, or forty.

• RIDICULOUSLY SIMPLE DIRECTIONS

In this tablet you will find stories containing blank spaces where words are left out. One player, the READER, selects one of these stories. The READER does not tell anyone what the story is about. Instead, he/she asks the other players, the WRITERS, to give him/her words. These words are used to fill in the blank spaces in the story.

• TO PLAY

The READER asks each WRITER in turn to call out a word—an adjective or a noun or whatever the space calls for—and uses them to fill in the blank spaces in the story. The result is a MAD LIBS® game.

When the READER then reads the completed MAD LIBS® game to the other players, they will discover that they have written a story that is fantastic, screamingly funny, shocking, silly, crazy, or just plain dumb—depending upon which words each WRITER called out.

• EXAMPLE (*Before* and *After*)

" _____ !" he said _____
         EXCLAMATION   ADVERB

as he jumped into his convertible _____ and
                                                        NOUN

drove off with his _____ wife.
                              ADJECTIVE

" _____OUCH_____ !" he said _____HAPPILY_____
         EXCLAMATION   ADVERB

as he jumped into his convertible _____CAT_____ and
                                                        NOUN

drove off with his _____BRAVE_____ wife.
                              ADJECTIVE

MAD LIBS®
QUICK REVIEW

In case you have forgotten what adjectives, adverbs, nouns, and verbs are, here is a quick review:

An ADJECTIVE describes something or somebody. *Lumpy, soft, ugly, messy,* and *short* are adjectives.

An ADVERB tells how something is done. It modifies a verb and usually ends in "ly." *Modestly, stupidly, greedily,* and *carefully* are adverbs.

A NOUN is the name of a person, place, or thing. *Sidewalk, umbrella, bridle, bathtub,* and *nose* are nouns.

A VERB is an action word. *Run, pitch, jump,* and *swim* are verbs. Put the verbs in past tense if the directions say PAST TENSE. *Ran, pitched, jumped,* and *swam* are verbs in the past tense.

When we ask for A PLACE, we mean any sort of place: a country or city (*Spain, Cleveland*) or a room (*bathroom, kitchen*).

An EXCLAMATION or SILLY WORD is any sort of funny sound, gasp, grunt, or outcry, like *Wow!, Ouch!, Whomp!, Ick!,* and *Gadzooks!*

When we ask for specific words, like a NUMBER, a COLOR, an ANIMAL, or a PART OF THE BODY, we mean a word that is one of those things, like *seven, blue, horse,* or *head.*

When we ask for a PLURAL, it means more than one. For example, *cat* pluralized is *cats.*

MAD LIBS® is fun to play with friends, but you can also play it by yourself! To begin with, DO NOT look at the story on the page below. Fill in the blanks on this page with the words called for. Then, using the words you have selected, fill in the blank spaces in the story.

Now you've created your own hilarious MAD LIBS® game!

HAPPY HALLOWEEN!

NOUN _____

PLURAL NOUN _____

OCCUPATION (PLURAL) _____

VERB _____

PLURAL NOUN _____

SILLY WORD _____

VERB ENDING IN "ING" _____

A PLACE _____

PLURAL NOUN _____

NOUN _____

SOMETHING ALIVE _____

VERB ENDING IN "ING" _____

TYPE OF FOOD _____

TYPE OF CONTAINER (PLURAL) _____

VERB _____

PART OF THE BODY _____

EXCLAMATION _____

MAD LIBS

HAPPY HALLOWEEN!

Halloween is the best _____ of the year! I can't wait to dress
                        NOUN

up in scary _____ with my friends. This year, we're all
             PLURAL NOUN

being zombie _____ so we can _____ people in
             OCCUPATION (PLURAL)   VERB

the neighborhood. I'm wearing rotting green _____ on my
                                             PLURAL NOUN

face and will moan "_____" everywhere I go. The best
                    SILLY WORD

part of Halloween is going trick-or- _____ around
                                      VERB ENDING IN "ING"

(the) _____ . Once night comes, we knock on people's
       A PLACE

_____ . When someone answers, we all shout
      PLURAL NOUN

"_____ or treat!" It's really fun when the _____
      NOUN   SOMETHING ALIVE

_____ the door gives us some sweet _____ .
VERB ENDING IN "ING"   TYPE OF FOOD

Then, we all slowly zombie-walk home with our pumpkin-shaped

_____ full of candy. I just wish zombies would
TYPE OF CONTAINER (PLURAL)

learn to not _____ all the candy at once so we don't end up
              VERB

with a/an _____ -ache. _____!
           PART OF THE BODY   EXCLAMATION

MAD LIBS® is fun to play with friends, but you can also play it by yourself! To begin with, DO NOT look at the story on the page below. Fill in the blanks on this page with the words called for. Then, using the words you have selected, fill in the blank spaces in the story.

Now you've created your own hilarious MAD LIBS® game!

BAG OR BUCKET?

VERB ENDING IN "ING" _____

TYPE OF FOOD _____

OCCUPATION (PLURAL) _____

ADJECTIVE _____

COLOR _____

ADJECTIVE _____

A PLACE _____

NOUN _____

NOUN _____

ADVERB _____

NUMBER _____

VERB _____

NOUN _____

VERB _____

TYPE OF FOOD _____

A PLACE (PLURAL) _____

NOUN _____

ADJECTIVE _____

Halloween is all about _____ candy! Here are some tips
VERB ENDING IN "ING"

to help you get as much _____ as you can from all the
TYPE OF FOOD

_____ in your neighborhood. The most important thing
OCCUPATION (PLURAL)

to do is pick out a/an _____ candy bucket. Usually they're
ADJECTIVE

shaped like a/an _____ pumpkin. But if you really want to be
COLOR

a/an _____ trick-or-treater, go to your _____ and get
ADJECTIVE   A PLACE

a pillow-_____ from your bed. Of course, you'll need to take
NOUN

out the comfy _____ to make room for all your candy, but it's
NOUN

_____ worth it. A pillowcase can hold _____
ADVERB   NUMBER

pounds more candy than you could ever _____ in a/an
VERB

_____! Then _____ the pavement and start demanding
NOUN   VERB

_____! Go to as many _____ as you can and shout
TYPE OF FOOD   A PLACE (PLURAL)

"trick or _____!" before the night is _____!
NOUN   ADJECTIVE

MAD LIBS® is fun to play with friends, but you can also play it by yourself! To begin with, DO NOT look at the story on the page below. Fill in the blanks on this page with the words called for. Then, using the words you have selected, fill in the blank spaces in the story.

Now you've created your own hilarious MAD LIBS® game!

NO COSTUME?
NO PROBLEM!

NOUN _____

ADJECTIVE _____

ADJECTIVE _____

NOUN _____

PART OF THE BODY _____

PART OF THE BODY _____

VERB _____

OCCUPATION _____

PLURAL NOUN _____

NOUN _____

ADJECTIVE _____

NOUN _____

NOUN _____

ANIMAL _____

ARTICLE OF CLOTHING _____

TYPE OF FOOD _____

TYPE OF LIQUID _____

MAD LIBS®
NO COSTUME?
NO PROBLEM!

So, you forgot to buy a/an _____ for Halloween this year?
NOUN

Here are some _____ costume ideas to make your night of
ADJECTIVE

trick-or-treating _____!
ADJECTIVE

- If you want to be a ghost, just get a/an _____ from your
NOUN

  bedroom and put it over your _____. Don't forget to
PART OF THE BODY

  cut _____-holes or you won't be able to _____.
PART OF THE BODY   VERB

- It's easy to be an ancient _____. Just get some stretchy
OCCUPATION

  _____ and wrap your entire _____ until it's
PLURAL NOUN   NOUN

  completely covered.

- If you want to trick-or-treat as a/an _____ vampire, get a
ADJECTIVE

  black _____ from your linen closet and wear it as a spooky
NOUN

  _____.
NOUN

- Want to be a headless _____-man? Just button your
ANIMAL

  _____ over your head and add some _____
ARTICLE OF CLOTHING   TYPE OF FOOD

  on the collar to look like _____.
TYPE OF LIQUID

MAD LIBS® is fun to play with friends, but you can also play it by yourself! To begin with, DO NOT look at the story on the page below. Fill in the blanks on this page with the words called for. Then, using the words you have selected, fill in the blank spaces in the story.

Now you've created your own hilarious MAD LIBS® game!

HALLOWEEN
WINNERS AND LOSERS

CELEBRITY _____

VERB ENDING IN "ING" _____

ADJECTIVE _____

A PLACE _____

NOUN _____

ANIMAL _____

ADJECTIVE _____

VERB _____

OCCUPATION _____

TYPE OF FOOD _____

VERB (PAST TENSE) _____

PLURAL NOUN _____

ADJECTIVE _____

ADJECTIVE _____

TYPE OF FOOD (PLURAL) _____

PLURAL NOUN _____

TYPE OF FOOD (PLURAL) _____

ADJECTIVE _____

MAD LIBS®
HALLOWEEN
WINNERS AND LOSERS

Hello, my name is _____ . There's nothing I love more than
             CELEBRITY

_____ on a costume and going trick-or-treating!
VERB ENDING IN "ING"

This year, I got some pretty _____ candy! The owners of (the)
                              ADJECTIVE

_____ next door gave me a chocolate-covered _____
A PLACE   NOUN

shaped like a/an _____ . It looked so _____ , I
                 ANIMAL   ADJECTIVE

couldn't wait to get home and _____ it! My other next-door
                               VERB

_____ gave me the yummiest candy bar ever. It was covered
OCCUPATION

with crunchy _____ that _____ every time
             TYPE OF FOOD   VERB (PAST TENSE)

I took a bite. Of course, not all the _____ I got were
                                        PLURAL NOUN

_____ . There always seems to be that one house that gives
ADJECTIVE

out _____ _____ instead of candy. One
    ADJECTIVE   TYPE OF FOOD (PLURAL)

year, they gave everyone red _____ from a tree in their yard,
                             PLURAL NOUN

and this year they gave out slices of ripe _____
                                           TYPE OF FOOD (PLURAL)

because they said they wanted us to be " _____ ."
                                          ADJECTIVE

MAD LIBS® is fun to play with friends, but you can also play it by yourself! To begin with, DO NOT look at the story on the page below. Fill in the blanks on this page with the words called for. Then, using the words you have selected, fill in the blank spaces in the story.

Now you've created your own hilarious MAD LIBS® game!

TRICK OR TREAT TACTICS

ADJECTIVE _____

TYPE OF FOOD (PLURAL) _____

VERB (PAST TENSE) _____

NOUN _____

ADJECTIVE _____

ADJECTIVE _____

VERB _____

NUMBER _____

VERB ENDING IN "ING" _____

EXCLAMATION _____

PLURAL NOUN _____

PLURAL NOUN _____

FIRST NAME _____

TYPE OF FOOD _____

TYPE OF BUILDING _____

ADJECTIVE _____

SAME TYPE OF BUILDING _____

MAD LIBS®

TRICK OR TREAT TACTICS

Here are some _____ tips to get lots of _____
             ADJECTIVE   TYPE OF FOOD (PLURAL)

when you go trick-or-treating on Halloween:

- People love costumes that they've never _____ before.
                                         VERB (PAST TENSE)

  Choose to wear a/an _____ that's original and _____ .
                       NOUN   ADJECTIVE

- Try on your _____ costume ahead of time to be sure you
                 ADJECTIVE

  can _____ around easily. It won't be easy to walk if your
       VERB

  costume weighs _____ pounds or if you can't see where you're
              NUMBER

  _____ .
  VERB ENDING IN "ING"

- Be polite and say "_____!" after someone puts
                     EXCLAMATION

  _____ in your bag.
  PLURAL NOUN

- Go to a house with lots of Halloween _____ taped up
                                PLURAL NOUN

  all over it. Lots of _____-o'-lanterns are also a sure
                   FIRST NAME

  sign that there's _____ inside that house.
                 TYPE OF FOOD

- Never go to a/an _____ if the lights are
                      TYPE OF BUILDING

  _____ . This either means no one's home or that it's a
  ADJECTIVE

  haunted _____ .
            SAME TYPE OF BUILDING

MAD LIBS® is fun to play with friends, but you can also play it by yourself! To begin with, DO NOT look at the story on the page below. Fill in the blanks on this page with the words called for. Then, using the words you have selected, fill in the blank spaces in the story.

Now you've created your own hilarious MAD LIBS® game!

HALLOWEEN TIME MACHINE

ADJECTIVE _____

SILLY WORD _____

OCCUPATION _____

NOUN _____

ADJECTIVE _____

NUMBER _____

ADJECTIVE _____

VERB _____

A PLACE _____

PLURAL NOUN _____

TYPE OF FOOD _____

ADJECTIVE _____

ADJECTIVE _____

VERB _____

NOUN _____

TYPE OF FOOD (PLURAL) _____

EXCLAMATION _____

ADJECTIVE _____

Here's a/an _____ interview with the world's oldest trick-or-
         ADJECTIVE
treater:

Interviewer: Hello, today I'm talking with Olga von _____,
                                                        SILLY WORD
the world's oldest _____ . Tell me, Olga, what was Halloween
                    OCCUPATION
like when you were a young _____ ?
                            NOUN

Olga: Oh, very, very _____ ! _____ years ago, when I
                         ADJECTIVE   NUMBER
was _____ , instead of walking from house to house, you had
     ADJECTIVE
to _____ from farm to _____ . I had to walk over
    VERB   A PLACE
twenty _____ in one night just to get two pieces of
        PLURAL NOUN
_____ .
TYPE OF FOOD

Interviewer: Wow. That sounds absolutely _____ !
                                              ADJECTIVE

Olga: And that's not even the _____ part. Instead of carrying
                                   ADJECTIVE
a plastic pumpkin, you had to _____ a heavy wooden
                               VERB
_____ , and people only handed out stale _____ .
NOUN   TYPE OF FOOD (PLURAL)

Interviewer: _____ . It sounds like kids today don't know
                  EXCLAMATION
how _____ they are!
     ADJECTIVE

MAD LIBS® is fun to play with friends, but you can also play it by yourself! To begin with, DO NOT look at the story on the page below. Fill in the blanks on this page with the words called for. Then, using the words you have selected, fill in the blank spaces in the story.

Now you've created your own hilarious MAD LIBS® game!

ALIEN REPORT!

VERB ENDING IN "ING" _____

EXCLAMATION _____

SILLY WORD _____

ADJECTIVE _____

NOUN _____

SOMETHING ALIVE (PLURAL) _____

ARTICLE OF CLOTHING (PLURAL) _____

PART OF THE BODY (PLURAL) _____

ADJECTIVE _____

VERB _____

ADJECTIVE _____

ANIMAL (PLURAL) _____

NOUN _____

PLURAL NOUN _____

PART OF THE BODY _____

VEHICLE _____

VERB _____

VERB ENDING IN "ING" _____

MAD LIBS®

ALIEN REPORT!

An alien who is _____ Halloween reports back to her
_____ VERB ENDING IN "ING"

home planet:

Gleeglorg: _____ , Grand Commander _____ .
_____ EXCLAMATION _____ SILLY WORD

I'm reporting my findings on the _____ Earth holiday called
_____ ADJECTIVE

Halloween. On this _____ , small _____
_____ NOUN _____ SOMETHING ALIVE (PLURAL)

like to take the _____ from a different creature
_____ ARTICLE OF CLOTHING (PLURAL)

and put them on their own _____ .
_____ PART OF THE BODY (PLURAL)

Fleeflorg: Hmmm. That's very _____ behavior.
_____ ADJECTIVE

Gleeglorg: Then they _____ in the dark to houses with
_____ VERB

many _____ skeletons and were- _____ placed in
___ ADJECTIVE _____ ANIMAL (PLURAL)

the front yard.

Fleeflorg: Thank you for your _____ , Gleeglorg. This report
_____ NOUN

is sending _____ down my _____ . Return to
___ PLURAL NOUN _____ PART OF THE BODY

the safety of your space _____ at once.
_____ VEHICLE

Gleeglorg: As you _____ , Grand Commander.
_____ VERB

_____ transmission.
__ VERB ENDING IN "ING"

MAD LIBS® is fun to play with friends, but you can also play it by yourself! To begin with, DO NOT look at the story on the page below. Fill in the blanks on this page with the words called for. Then, using the words you have selected, fill in the blank spaces in the story.

Now you've created your own hilarious MAD LIBS® game!

DEVIOUS DECORATING

ADJECTIVE _____

VERB ENDING IN "ING" _____

ADJECTIVE _____

A PLACE _____

ADJECTIVE _____

PLURAL NOUN _____

PART OF THE BODY (PLURAL) _____

SOMETHING ALIVE (PLURAL) _____

VERB _____

VERB _____

PLURAL NOUN _____

SOMETHING ALIVE (PLURAL) _____

ADJECTIVE _____

NOUN _____

EXCLAMATION _____

VERB _____

TYPE OF FOOD (PLURAL) _____

PLURAL NOUN _____

MAD LIBS®
DEVIOUS DECORATING

On Halloween, you want your house to look as _____ as
                                            ADJECTIVE
possible to scare the trick-or-treaters who come _____
                                                 VERB ENDING IN "ING"
for candy. One _____ idea is to turn your front yard into a
                ADJECTIVE
haunted _____ . You can do this by making _____
         A PLACE   ADJECTIVE
tombstones out of cardboard _____ and placing them
                              PLURAL NOUN
around the yard. Then add plastic _____ sticking
                                   PART OF THE BODY (PLURAL)
out of the dirt in front of the tombstones so it looks like spooky

_____ are trying to _____ their way to the
SOMETHING ALIVE (PLURAL)   VERB
surface and _____ the trick-or-treaters. Next, hang as many
             VERB
spider- _____ as you can from the _____
         PLURAL NOUN   SOMETHING ALIVE (PLURAL)
and bushes, and play _____ music. When the trick-or-treaters
                      ADJECTIVE
come, jump out from behind a/an _____ and shout
                                 NOUN
" _____ !" This should make the trick-or-treaters
   EXCLAMATION
_____ , but don't worry: They'll feel better once you put
 VERB
_____ in their _____ .
TYPE OF FOOD (PLURAL)   PLURAL NOUN

MAD LIBS® is fun to play with friends, but you can also play it by yourself! To begin with, DO NOT look at the story on the page below. Fill in the blanks on this page with the words called for. Then, using the words you have selected, fill in the blank spaces in the story.

Now you've created your own hilarious MAD LIBS® game!

TREAT *AND* TRICK!

OCCUPATION _____

ADJECTIVE _____

TYPE OF BUILDING _____

NOUN _____

ARTICLE OF CLOTHING _____

TYPE OF FOOD (PLURAL) _____

ADVERB _____

VERB (PAST TENSE) _____

ADJECTIVE _____

ANIMAL _____

PART OF THE BODY (PLURAL) _____

NOUN _____

VERB _____

PART OF THE BODY _____

PART OF THE BODY _____

EXCLAMATION _____

VERB ENDING IN "ING" _____

VERB _____

MAD LIBS

TREAT *AND* TRICK!

Last Halloween, my best _____ and I went trick-or-treating
<small>OCCUPATION</small>

at a/an _____ _____. All the kids in the
<small>ADJECTIVE</small>   <small>TYPE OF BUILDING</small>

neighborhood thought the woman who lived there was a wicked

_____. But we hoped she was just wearing a really good
<small>NOUN</small>

Halloween _____. The witch gave us some strange
<small>ARTICLE OF CLOTHING</small>

_____ to eat. My best friend _____
<small>TYPE OF FOOD (PLURAL)</small>   <small>ADVERB</small>

_____ the treats and then something _____
<small>VERB (PAST TENSE)</small>   <small>ADJECTIVE</small>

happened—he turned into a/an _____, right in front of my
<small>ANIMAL</small>

_____! At first, I thought this was just some type of
<small>PART OF THE BODY (PLURAL)</small>

magic _____, but then he started to _____ like a
<small>NOUN</small>   <small>VERB</small>

frog, too. He even grabbed my _____ and tried to bite my
<small>PART OF THE BODY</small>

_____. " _____!" I shouted, before
<small>PART OF THE BODY</small>   <small>EXCLAMATION</small>

_____ down the street. That's the last time I ever
<small>VERB ENDING IN "ING"</small>

_____ on a witch's door.
<small>VERB</small>

MAD LIBS® is fun to play with friends, but you can also play it by yourself! To begin with, DO NOT look at the story on the page below. Fill in the blanks on this page with the words called for. Then, using the words you have selected, fill in the blank spaces in the story.

Now you've created your own hilarious MAD LIBS® game!

CREEPY TREATS

ADJECTIVE _____

TYPE OF BUILDING _____

VERB _____

COLOR _____

PART OF THE BODY (PLURAL) _____

ADJECTIVE _____

ANIMAL (PLURAL) _____

PART OF THE BODY (PLURAL) _____

ADJECTIVE _____

VERB _____

VERB _____

PART OF THE BODY (PLURAL) _____

COLOR _____

TYPE OF FOOD (PLURAL) _____

NOUN _____

NOUN _____

MAD LIBS®

CREEPY TREATS

One of the _____ things about Halloween is making
ADJECTIVE

_____-made treats. Here are some ideas that'll make
TYPE OF BUILDING

kids _____ with joy!
VERB

• Bake _____ cookies with lots of _____
COLOR   PART OF THE BODY (PLURAL)

so they look like _____ black widow _____ .
ADJECTIVE   ANIMAL (PLURAL)

• Attach a pair of paper _____ to the sides of a
PART OF THE BODY (PLURAL)

cupcake to make it look like a/an _____ bat, ready to
ADJECTIVE

_____ through the sky!
VERB

• You can _____ broken candy canes into a vampire cookie
VERB

so they look like sharp _____ .
PART OF THE BODY (PLURAL)

• Take a/an _____ apple and dip it in melted white
COLOR

_____ . Then push a/an _____ into the
TYPE OF FOOD (PLURAL)   NOUN

center and serve it upside down as a ghostly _____ !
NOUN

MAD LIBS® is fun to play with friends, but you can also play it by yourself! To begin with, DO NOT look at the story on the page below. Fill in the blanks on this page with the words called for. Then, using the words you have selected, fill in the blank spaces in the story.

Now you've created your own hilarious MAD LIBS® game!

FRANKENSTEIN'S DIARY

VERB ENDING IN "ING" _____

ADJECTIVE _____

NOUN _____

PLURAL NOUN _____

SOMETHING ALIVE (PLURAL) _____

VERB ENDING IN "ING" _____

NOUN _____

TYPE OF EVENT _____

VERB _____

ADJECTIVE _____

TYPE OF FOOD (PLURAL) _____

SOMETHING ALIVE _____

ARTICLE OF CLOTHING _____

NOUN _____

PART OF THE BODY _____

SILLY WORD _____

PLURAL NOUN _____

NOUN _____

Dear Diary. Today me have fun and go trick-or- _____
                                              VERB ENDING IN "ING"

for first time. Good news is, face already look _____ , so me
                                                ADJECTIVE

not have to wear Halloween _____ . Me see kids dressed as
                            NOUN

_____ and _____ . No one afraid of me
PLURAL NOUN   SOMETHING ALIVE (PLURAL)

because they think me _____ fake _____ .
                       VERB ENDING IN "ING"   NOUN

Next, me go with kids to Halloween _____ . There,
                                    TYPE OF EVENT

everyone _____ to _____ music and play Halloween
          VERB   ADJECTIVE

games, like bobbing for _____ . Me have lots of
                         TYPE OF FOOD (PLURAL)

fun dancing with _____ . Then, me win best
                  SOMETHING ALIVE

_____ contest. When villagers try to take off me
ARTICLE OF CLOTHING

_____ , they realize it really me _____ . They
NOUN   PART OF THE BODY

scream " _____ !" and chase me away with pitchforks and
          SILLY WORD

_____ . Me love Halloween and next year me want to go
PLURAL NOUN

trick-or-treating dressed as a friendly _____ .
                                         NOUN

MAD LIBS® is fun to play with friends, but you can also play it by yourself! To begin with, DO NOT look at the story on the page below. Fill in the blanks on this page with the words called for. Then, using the words you have selected, fill in the blank spaces in the story.

Now you've created your own hilarious MAD LIBS® game!

TOIL AND TROUBLE

NOUN _____

PART OF THE BODY (PLURAL) _____

PART OF THE BODY _____

ANIMAL _____

NUMBER _____

NOUN _____

ADJECTIVE _____

TYPE OF LIQUID _____

TYPE OF FOOD (PLURAL) _____

VERB _____

NOUN _____

NUMBER _____

TYPE OF CONTAINER _____

VERB ENDING IN "ING" _____

NOUN _____

TOIL AND TROUBLE

Hello, fellow witches! Here's a recipe to whip up a wicked _____
NOUN

that'll put a smile on those pesky kids' _____ when
PART OF THE BODY (PLURAL)

they come to your door on Halloween.

1. Take one _____ of a/an _____ and mix it with
PART OF THE BODY   ANIMAL

_____ pinches of _____ .
NUMBER   NOUN

2. Pour in _____ _____ and blend until it smells
ADJECTIVE   TYPE OF LIQUID

like fried _____ .
TYPE OF FOOD (PLURAL)

3. _____ all the ingredients in an iron _____ .
VERB   NOUN

Once cooked, put _____ drops of the potion in a/an
NUMBER

_____ and give it to any child who comes to your
TYPE OF CONTAINER

door _____ for a yummy _____ .
VERB ENDING IN "ING"   NOUN

MAD LIBS® is fun to play with friends, but you can also play it by yourself! To begin with, DO NOT look at the story on the page below. Fill in the blanks on this page with the words called for. Then, using the words you have selected, fill in the blank spaces in the story.

Now you've created your own hilarious MAD LIBS® game!

HISTORY OF
TRICK-OR-TREATING

COUNTRY _____

NUMBER _____

VERB (PAST TENSE) _____

PLURAL NOUN _____

SILLY WORD _____

SAME SILLY WORD _____

PART OF THE BODY (PLURAL) _____

PLURAL NOUN _____

ADJECTIVE _____

TYPE OF FOOD (PLURAL) _____

TYPE OF LIQUID (PLURAL) _____

SOMETHING ALIVE (PLURAL) _____

VERB _____

ADJECTIVE _____

VERB _____

TYPE OF FOOD (PLURAL) _____

TYPE OF EVENT _____

MAD LIBS®
HISTORY OF
TRICK-OR-TREATING

Trick-or-treating is a custom that started in _____ nearly

COUNTRY

_____ years ago. The people who _____ during

NUMBER   VERB (PAST TENSE)

that time believed that creepy _____ returned to earth

PLURAL NOUN

once a year to cause mischief. They called this night _____.

SILLY WORD

As part of this event, the people created the festival of

_____. During the festival, villagers would dress themselves

SAME SILLY WORD

in animal _____ to drive away evil _____.

PART OF THE BODY (PLURAL)   PLURAL NOUN

_____ banquet tables were filled with delicious

ADJECTIVE

_____ and warm _____, and

TYPE OF FOOD (PLURAL)   TYPE OF LIQUID (PLURAL)

were meant to appease any hungry _____ that would

SOMETHING ALIVE (PLURAL)

_____ the earth on that _____ night. Centuries later,

VERB   ADJECTIVE

kids began to _____ from house to house and ask for

VERB

_____ to celebrate the same ritual. Today, this

TYPE OF FOOD (PLURAL)

custom is celebrated in places around the world as the _____

TYPE OF EVENT

of Halloween.

MAD LIBS® is fun to play with friends, but you can also play it by yourself! To begin with, DO NOT look at the story on the page below. Fill in the blanks on this page with the words called for. Then, using the words you have selected, fill in the blank spaces in the story.

Now you've created your own hilarious MAD LIBS® game!

CANDY COMMERCIAL

ADJECTIVE _____

SOMETHING ALIVE (PLURAL) _____

TYPE OF FOOD (PLURAL) _____

NOUN _____

SILLY WORD _____

VERB _____

NOUN _____

PART OF THE BODY (PLURAL) _____

TYPE OF FOOD (PLURAL) _____

NUMBER _____

TYPE OF FOOD (PLURAL) _____

NOUN _____

PART OF THE BODY _____

VERB _____

TYPE OF FOOD (PLURAL) _____

PLURAL NOUN _____

VERB (PAST TENSE) _____

MAD LIBS®

CANDY COMMERCIAL

Are you tired of handing out the same _____ candy every year
                                        ADJECTIVE

on Halloween? Do all the _____ skip your house
                          SOMETHING ALIVE (PLURAL)

when they trick-or-treat because the _____ you
                                     TYPE OF FOOD (PLURAL)

hand out are as tasty as an old _____? Well, come on down
                                NOUN

to Ted's _____ Candy Shop! Our candy experts lovingly
         SILLY WORD

_____ each delicious _____ with their own
VERB   NOUN

_____. All our _____ are covered
PART OF THE BODY (PLURAL)   TYPE OF FOOD (PLURAL)

in _____ percent yummy yumminess! And Ted's lollipops are
   NUMBER

filled with chewy _____ that'll let you blow the
                  TYPE OF FOOD (PLURAL)

biggest _____ you've ever seen! Once the trick-or-treaters see
        NOUN

you pull out one of our famous _____ -breakers,
                               PART OF THE BODY

they'll _____ with delight! One bite of any of our
        VERB

_____ and the kids in your neighborhood will say
TYPE OF FOOD (PLURAL)

your family hands out the best _____ they've ever
                               PLURAL NOUN

_____ .
VERB (PAST TENSE)

MAD LIBS® is fun to play with friends, but you can also play it by yourself! To begin with, DO NOT look at the story on the page below. Fill in the blanks on this page with the words called for. Then, using the words you have selected, fill in the blank spaces in the story.

Now you've created your own hilarious MAD LIBS® game!

EXPRESS YOURSELF!

VERB _____

VERB _____

PLURAL NOUN _____

PART OF THE BODY (PLURAL) _____

ADJECTIVE _____

ARTICLE OF CLOTHING _____

SILLY WORD _____

OCCUPATION _____

NOUN _____

VERB _____

ADJECTIVE _____

ARTICLE OF CLOTHING _____

PART OF THE BODY _____

NOUN _____

VERB _____

NOUN _____

VERB _____

PLURAL NOUN _____

MAD LIBS®

EXPRESS YOURSELF!

Halloween is a great chance to dress up as the thing you _____
                                                                VERB

most! It's a night when ghosts _____ the neighborhoods, and
                                      VERB

undead _____ roam the streets in search of human
            PLURAL NOUN

_____ to eat. Of course, not all costumes need to
PART OF THE BODY (PLURAL)

be _____ . If you want to be a cowboy, just put a/an
        ADJECTIVE

_____ on your head and shout "Yee-_____!"
ARTICLE OF CLOTHING   SILLY WORD

If you've always wanted to be a super-_____, put on a/an
                                            OCCUPATION

_____ and pretend you can _____ through the sky.
    NOUN   VERB

A princess is another _____ costume. If that's more your
                            ADJECTIVE

speed, just wear a long, flowing _____ and put a
                                      ARTICLE OF CLOTHING

crown on your _____ . You can even dress as something
                  PART OF THE BODY

silly, like a/an _____ , to make people _____ .
                    NOUN   VERB

Whatever _____ you choose to wear, just remember that the
              NOUN

most important thing is to _____ yourself and have a fun
                                VERB

night with your best _____!
                          PLURAL NOUN

MAD LIBS® is fun to play with friends, but you can also play it by yourself! To begin with, DO NOT look at the story on the page below. Fill in the blanks on this page with the words called for. Then, using the words you have selected, fill in the blank spaces in the story.

Now you've created your own hilarious MAD LIBS® game!

HOWLING BEAUTY

ADJECTIVE _____

VERB ENDING IN "ING" _____

SOMETHING ALIVE _____

PART OF THE BODY _____

NUMBER _____

ADJECTIVE _____

EXCLAMATION _____

PART OF THE BODY (PLURAL) _____

VERB _____

VERB _____

TYPE OF LIQUID _____

ADJECTIVE _____

VERB _____

ADJECTIVE _____

VERB _____

MAD LIBS®

HOWLING BEAUTY

Even a werewolf wants to look _____ when they go trick-
                               ADJECTIVE

or- _____ on Halloween night. Here are some helpful
     VERB ENDING IN "ING"

tips for the _____ in everyone!
              SOMETHING ALIVE

* Make sure to comb your _____ at least _____
                          PART OF THE BODY   NUMBER

  times so your fur is nice and _____ .
                                 ADJECTIVE

* Nothing says " _____ !" like bright, shiny
                            EXCLAMATION

  _____ ! So before you go out, use a toothbrush
  PART OF THE BODY (PLURAL)

  to _____ your fangs until they're gleaming white.
       VERB

* If you really want to _____ at the moon, make sure
                             VERB

  to drink plenty of warm _____ so your voice is
                             TYPE OF LIQUID

  _____ .
    ADJECTIVE

* And what werewolf doesn't love to _____ to some music?
                                          VERB

  Make sure you get some _____ shoes so you can
                              ADJECTIVE

  _____ the night away!
      VERB

MAD LIBS® is fun to play with friends, but you can also play it by yourself! To begin with, DO NOT look at the story on the page below. Fill in the blanks on this page with the words called for. Then, using the words you have selected, fill in the blank spaces in the story.

Now you've created your own hilarious MAD LIBS® game!

PUMPKIN IT UP

VERB ENDING IN "ING" _____

PLURAL NOUN _____

NOUN _____

PART OF THE BODY (PLURAL) _____

PART OF THE BODY _____

NOUN _____

ADJECTIVE _____

TYPE OF FOOD _____

ADJECTIVE _____

NOUN _____

PLURAL NOUN _____

PLURAL NOUN _____

ADJECTIVE _____

NOUN _____

NOUN _____

VERB _____

NOUN _____

MAD LIBS®

PUMPKIN IT UP

Check out these steps for _____ a pumpkin that will
                          VERB ENDING IN "ING"

scare the _____ that come to your _____ on
          PLURAL NOUN   NOUN

Halloween:

1. Once you've selected your pumpkin, use a marker to draw

   _____ and a/an _____ on the
   PART OF THE BODY (PLURAL)   PART OF THE BODY

   pumpkin's _____ . Some people like to carve a/an
             NOUN

   _____ face, while others prefer making the _____
   ADJECTIVE   TYPE OF FOOD

   look silly.

2. Next, ask an adult to get a/an _____ _____ ,
                                   ADJECTIVE   NOUN

   so they can carefully cut the pumpkin along the marker lines.

   Remove the pumpkin's inner _____ and clean out all
                              PLURAL NOUN

   the sticky _____ growing inside.
              PLURAL NOUN

3. Light up your jack-o'-lantern with a/an _____ glow
                                           ADJECTIVE

   by putting a battery-operated _____ inside the pumpkin,
                                 NOUN

   then place the pumpkin on your _____ . Finally, sit
                                  NOUN

   back and _____ your scary _____ !
            VERB   NOUN

MAD LIBS® is fun to play with friends, but you can also play it by yourself! To begin with, DO NOT look at the story on the page below. Fill in the blanks on this page with the words called for. Then, using the words you have selected, fill in the blank spaces in the story.

Now you've created your own hilarious MAD LIBS® game!

TRICK OR TREAT SAFETY TIPS

NOUN _____

ADJECTIVE _____

ADVERB _____

VERB ENDING IN "S" _____

PLURAL NOUN _____

VERB ENDING IN "ING" _____

NOUN _____

PLURAL NOUN _____

VEHICLE (PLURAL) _____

OCCUPATION _____

VERB _____

PLURAL NOUN _____

NOUN _____

VERB _____

TYPE OF BUILDING (PLURAL) _____

TYPE OF FOOD _____

MAD LIBS®
TRICK OR TREAT
SAFETY TIPS

Here is a step-by-_____ guide to help you stay safe and
NOUN
_____ on Halloween night!
ADJECTIVE

• Make sure your Halloween costume fits and is zipped up

  _____ . No one wants to be the mummy who
  ADVERB

  _____ over their own _____ .
  VERB ENDING IN "S"   _PLURAL NOUN_

• Since you'll be _____ in the dark, carry a bright
  VERB ENDING IN "ING"

  _____ with you. That way you can see any _____
  NOUN   _PLURAL NOUN_

  in your path, and you can be seen by passing _____ .
  VEHICLE (PLURAL)

• Take a parent or _____ with you, and always
  OCCUPATION

  _____ in a group. Halloween is more fun with a group of
  VERB

  _____ anyway!
  PLURAL NOUN

• Use a/an _____ to plan your route and _____ the
  NOUN   _VERB_

  _____ in your neighborhood early. That way,
  TYPE OF BUILDING (PLURAL)

  you'll have enough time to count your _____ before
  TYPE OF FOOD

  bedtime.

MAD LIBS® is fun to play with friends, but you can also play it by yourself! To begin with, DO NOT look at the story on the page below. Fill in the blanks on this page with the words called for. Then, using the words you have selected, fill in the blank spaces in the story.

Now you've created your own hilarious MAD LIBS® game!

HALLOVEEN BITES!

SILLY WORD _____

SOMETHING ALIVE _____

VERB _____

VERB _____

PLURAL NOUN _____

A PLACE (PLURAL) _____

PLURAL NOUN _____

TYPE OF FOOD (PLURAL) _____

ADJECTIVE _____

PART OF THE BODY _____

ADJECTIVE _____

ANIMAL _____

PART OF THE BODY (PLURAL) _____

NOUN _____

PART OF THE BODY (PLURAL) _____

NOUN _____

VERB (PAST TENSE) _____

CELEBRITY _____

MAD LIBS®

HALLOVEEN BITES!

Good evening. I am the vampire Count _____ . You vould

SILLY WORD

think that because I'm a/an _____ of the night,

SOMETHING ALIVE

Halloveen vould be my favorite time of year. But the truth is, vampires

_____ Halloveen! Usually, when people see me, they

VERB

_____ and run avay! But on Halloveen, children dressed as

VERB

_____ vander (the) _____ , holding out

PLURAL NOUN   A PLACE (PLURAL)

their little hands, demanding _____ . If I do not give

PLURAL NOUN

them _____ , they pull a trick on me, like pouring

TYPE OF FOOD (PLURAL)

something _____ on my _____ . One time

ADJECTIVE   PART OF THE BODY

I became so _____ , I turned into a/an _____

ADJECTIVE   ANIMAL

and tried to bite their _____ . "I vant to

PART OF THE BODY (PLURAL)

suck your _____ ," I hissed as I showed them

NOUN

my _____ . But the dreadful little children thought

PART OF THE BODY (PLURAL)

I vas just vearing a/an _____ , and they _____

NOUN   VERB (PAST TENSE)

at me! On nights like these, I vish I vas _____ instead

CELEBRITY

of a vampire.

MAD LIBS® is fun to play with friends, but you can also play it by yourself! To begin with, DO NOT look at the story on the page below. Fill in the blanks on this page with the words called for. Then, using the words you have selected, fill in the blank spaces in the story.

Now you've created your own hilarious MAD LIBS® game!

HALLOWEEN MOVIE MADNESS

VERB _____

NOUN _____

NOUN _____

ADJECTIVE _____

VERB _____

PLURAL NOUN _____

TYPE OF FOOD _____

SOMETHING ALIVE _____

VERB ENDING IN "ING" _____

VERB _____

PLURAL NOUN _____

VERB _____

A PLACE (PLURAL) _____

CELEBRITY _____

LAST NAME _____

CELEBRITY _____

PERSON IN ROOM _____

MAD LIBS®
HALLOWEEN MOVIE MADNESS

Do you dare to _____ the most frightening movie of the year:
                     VERB

Night of the Living _____? It's the Halloween horror
                            NOUN

_____ you've been waiting for! Follow the _____
      NOUN   ADJECTIVE

story of three best friends as they _____ around their
                                           VERB

neighborhood on Halloween. What starts out as a fun evening turns

into a nightmare of epic _____ when the friends unwrap
                               PLURAL NOUN

a Halloween _____ and discover an evil _____
            TYPE OF FOOD   SOMETHING ALIVE

_____ inside! You'll never _____ with the
  VERB ENDING IN "ING"   VERB

lights off again after seeing the trick-or-treaters in a haunted house

filled with possessed _____! These three unfortunate friends
                       PLURAL NOUN

must _____ for their lives if they ever hope to see their
         VERB

_____ again! Starring _____ as
     A PLACE (PLURAL)   CELEBRITY

Karen _____ and _____ in the role of a lifetime
       LAST NAME   CELEBRITY

as _____ .
    PERSON IN ROOM

From TRICK OR TREAT MAD LIBS® • Copyright © 2020 by Penguin Random House LLC

MAD LIBS® is fun to play with friends, but you can also play it by yourself! To begin with, DO NOT look at the story on the page below. Fill in the blanks on this page with the words called for. Then, using the words you have selected, fill in the blank spaces in the story.

Now you've created your own hilarious MAD LIBS® game!

TREATS AND NO TRICKS

NOUN _____

ADJECTIVE _____

NOUN _____

NOUN _____

ADJECTIVE _____

VERB ENDING IN "ING" _____

VERB _____

NOUN _____

VERB ENDING IN "S" _____

TYPE OF LIQUID _____

VERB _____

TYPE OF FOOD _____

PART OF THE BODY _____

VERB _____

NOUN _____

MAD LIBS
TREATS AND NO TRICKS

Sometimes it's hard to tell if a trick-or-treater is just wearing a/an

_____ or if they are the real thing! Here's a/an _____
NOUN   ADJECTIVE

quiz to see if you can tell the difference between what's real and what's

a/an _____!
         NOUN

1. The best way to tell if a wizard is real, and not just a/an

   _____ in a costume, is to: (a) play _____ music
         NOUN   ADJECTIVE

   and see if they start _____ or (b) ask them to
                          VERB ENDING IN "ING"

   _____ a spell with their magical _____.
         VERB   NOUN

2. If you meet someone who _____ like a vampire,
                             VERB ENDING IN "S"

   you should: (a) throw cold _____ on them and see if they
                               TYPE OF LIQUID

   _____ or (b) rub some _____ on their
          VERB   TYPE OF FOOD

   _____, since real vampires _____ garlic.
   PART OF THE BODY   VERB

If you guessed *b* for both questions, congratulations—you can tell the

real thing from a/an _____!
                          NOUN